Capsized!

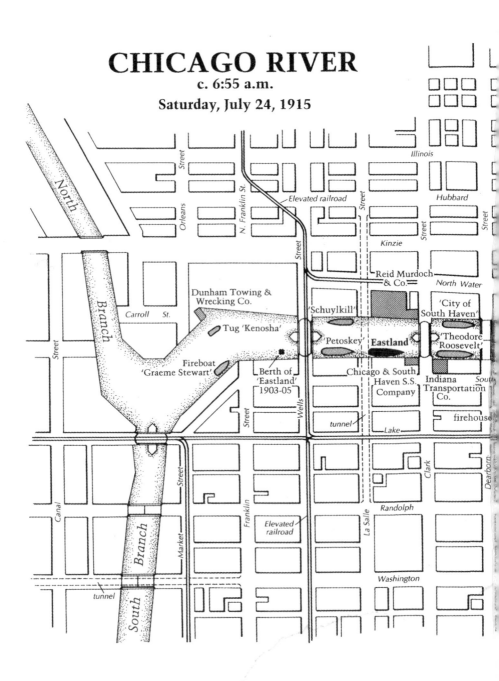

CHICAGO RIVER
c. 6:55 a.m.
Saturday, July 24, 1915

Illinois

North

Street

Orleans

N. Franklin St.

Elevated railroad

Street

Hubbard

Street

Kinzie

Street

Reid Murdoch
& Co.

North Water

Dunham Towing &
Wrecking Co.

Branch

Carroll St.

'Schuylkill'

'City of
South Haven'

Tug 'Kenosha'

'Petoskey'

Eastland

'Theodore
Roosevelt'

Street

Fireboat
'Graeme Stewart'

Berth of
'Eastland'
1903-05

Chicago & South
Haven S.S.
Company

Indiana
Transportation
Co.

Sout

Wells

tunnel

Lake

firehouse

Clark

Dearborn

Street

Canal

Franklin

La Salle

Randolph

Elevated
railroad

South Branch

Market

Washington

tunnel

Street

Street
Street
Street
Street

Cass
Rush
Pine

Street

Street
Street

Street

Street

Hill Steamboat
Co.
? 'Maywood'
Michigan Canal

Northern Michigan
Transportation
Co.
Water Street
'Illinois,' 'Missouri,' 'Rochester'
(relative position uncertain)

North

'Christopher Columbus'

Lake Michigan
1200 feet

River

Goodrich
Transit Co.

Slip A
Slip B
Slip C

Chicago

'Racine'
?
'Puritan'
River

'United
States'
Water

Avenue

'Indiana,'
'Georgia,' 'Alabama'
(relative position
uncertain)

Graham & Morton
Transportation
Company

Street

Street

State

Avenue

Michigan

Street

Wabash

Street

0   400   800   1200   1600
feet

CAPSIZED!

The Forgotten Story of the SS *Eastland* Disaster

PATRICIA SUTTON

The Library of Congress has cataloged the hardcover edition as follows:
Names: Sutton, Patricia, author.
Title: Capsized! : the forgotten story of the SS Eastland disaster / Patricia
    Sutton.
Description: Chicago, Illinois : Chicago Review Press, 2018. | Includes
    bibliographical references and index. | Audience: Age 10+ | Audience:
    Grade 4 to 6. |
Identifiers: LCCN 2017051163 (print) | LCCN 2018007087 (ebook) | ISBN
    9781613739440 (adobe pdf) | ISBN 9781613739457 (kindle) | ISBN
    9781613739464 (epub) | ISBN 9781613739433 (hardback)
Subjects: LCSH: Eastland (Ship)—Juvenile literature. |
    Shipwrecks—Illinois—Chicago River—Juvenile literature. | BISAC:
    JUVENILE NONFICTION / History / United States / 20th Century. |
    JUVENILE
    NONFICTION / History / United States / State & Local.
Classification: LCC G530.E18 (ebook) | LCC G530.E18 S87 2018 (print) |
    DDC
    917.73/110441—dc23
LC record available at https://lccn.loc.gov/2017051163

Cover design: Jonathan Hahn
Front cover illustration: Rick Tuma
Interior design: Sarah Olson

Printed in the United States of America

—— · ——

Dedicated to the memory of the 844

—— · ——

CONTENTS

—— . ——

MAIN CHARACTERS

———— · ————

Borghild "Bobbie" Aanstad—A 13-year-old girl headed to the Western Electric employee picnic, along with her sister Solveig, mother Marianne, and uncle Olaf Ness

Kelly family—New arrivals to Western Electric in Chicago: Charles Kelly, wife Mamie, nine-year-old Jenny, and five-year-old Charlie

Thyer family—Neighbors of the Kellys: Western Electric employee Henry Thyer, wife Helen, nine-year-old Helen, and seven-year-old Harry

Goyette family—George, foreman of the Woodworking Department at Western Electric, and three of his sons—Lyle, Frank, and Charlie

Working girls—The Polivka and Zastera sisters, Helen Greszowiak, and Emma Grossman—a few of the hundreds of single female employees scheduled to march in the picnic's beauty parade

Number 396—An eight-year-old boy with brown hair, a full face, and a broad nose

CREW

Captain Harry Pedersen—Veteran captain serving aboard the SS *Eastland*

Chief Engineer Joseph Erickson—Newly hired officer aboard the *Eastland*

RESPONDERS

Helen Repa—Western Electric nurse assigned to staff the hospital tent for the picnic

PROLOGUE

——— · ———

Promising to be the fastest steamship to sail the Great
Lakes, the SS *Eastland* drew the families of Port Huron,
Michigan, to the banks of the Black River on May 6,
1903. On a Tuesday afternoon, shops and offices around
town closed, and a school holiday sent children stream-
ing into the streets at noon. Buildings were draped in
red, white, and blue bunting, a brass band played Sousa
marches, and curious onlookers climbed trees or sat on
the roofs of nearby buildings for a better look. More
than 6,000 citizens turned out to witness the launch of
the first passenger ship built by the Jenks Shipbuilding
Company. After watching eight months of progress on
the town's newest vessel, they came to celebrate the
send-off.

At precisely 2:15 PM, two sharp blasts sounded from
the ship and the *Eastland* began to awaken, moving

just a bit, shifting and stirring from a still position. Factory whistles shrieked, tugboat horns blared, and church bells rang out to herald the moment. The captain's wife, Mrs. Frances Pereue, stepped forward and "struck a beribboned bottle of champagne against her steel bow."

As the crowd clapped and cheered, the *Eastland* slid sideways down the rails into the river, sending a cascade of water splashing to the shore. The ship rolled to a 45-degree angle and stopped, holding a precarious lean. People gasped, watching and waiting to see what would happen next.

Then the *Eastland* righted itself to the roar of the excited spectators.

The *Eastland* at the Jenks shipyard.

Launch of a Great Lakes steamship.

"She came right back up, just as nice and steady as a church," remarked shipbuilder Sidney Jenks. "Steady as a church."

A year later, on a sweltering summer evening, the *Eastland* transported its cargo of tired picnickers home to Chicago, from the beaches of South Haven, Michigan.

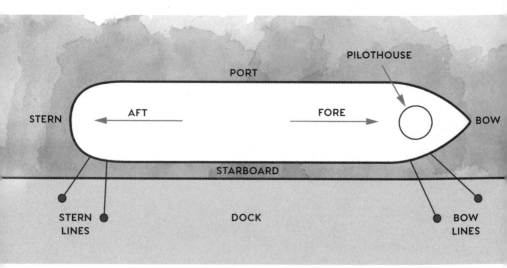

Nautical terms and diagram of the *Eastland* at the pier.

July 14, 1904, was the hottest day on record, and nearly half of the 2,300 passengers packed the upper hurricane deck, hoping for a cool lake breeze.

Captain Frank Dority headed full speed toward Chicago, but only a mile and half from the Michigan shore the *Eastland* suddenly tilted to the left, or port, side. In the engine room, chief engineer William Eeles estimated a 15-degree lean and knew that he had to use the large ballast tanks at the bottom of the ship to straighten it. First, he had to empty water from tanks number 1 and 2. Then he opened the valves on the opposite side of the lean, the starboard side, and lake water gushed into tank number 4. The weight of the water should have balanced the *Eastland*, bringing the ship to an even keel.

But nothing happened.

Screaming passengers scrambled to the high side of the ship, slipping and falling and reaching for anything to hold on to—a railing, a bench, a wall.

"Grab the life preservers!" someone hollered.

For nearly 10 minutes, the *Eastland* continued its lean and the engineer struggled to gain control. Crew members' faces turned pale and serious, and Captain Dority grew more impatient with the passing of each minute.

Frantic to reverse the listing, a nautical term for leaning, Eeles ran through his actions. Yes, he had first emptied the tanks of water. Yes, he had then opened

The SS *Eastland* at full steam.

valves on the starboard side for nearly five minutes. He waited and watched. Then slowly, the *Eastland* rolled back to center, balancing out. He breathed a sigh of relief. But almost immediately after settling, the ship seesawed in the opposite direction, this time creating an even steeper incline to starboard.

"Engines in check!" ordered Captain Dority. His first mate followed directions and immediately reduced the speed by half. The captain turned over the ship's wheel to his assistant and stormed out of the pilothouse, racing below to the engine room.

Shrieks pierced the evening air with the sudden shift, and passengers once again rushed to climb the steep deck to the opposite side. In the crush, many were shoved, several became seasick, some dropped to their knees to pray. Passengers fainted, and children screamed as they lost their grip and tumbled down the incline. One panicked woman nearly jumped overboard, saved by a stranger who grabbed her just in time. The sound of rushing water came from below.

Crew members headed down to try to close the open portholes on the lower decks. But it was too late. On the main deck, the lake water surged through gangway doors, flooding the bar, knocking over passengers, and pushing them against the hull.

Upon reaching the engine room, Dority demanded answers. The engineer tried to explain that there had been a problem with one of the tanks but that he believed it was corrected. They agreed that the number of people on the upper deck was not helping the situation.

Captain Dority rushed to the crowded hurricane deck, now top-heavy with passengers.

"The list will grow no worse," he explained, "if you will go below." Many still clung to the railings of the upper decks, afraid to go inside and be trapped if the boat capsized. The crew tried to persuade the crowd to follow the captain's orders. The *Chicago Tribune* reported that "the passengers refused to obey orders, and finally in order to drive them away from the rail, the fire hose was used." Passengers huddled together belowdecks, securing soggy life preservers, holding tight to loved ones, and anticipating the worst.

After nearly 25 minutes of rolling and lurching, the *Eastland* finally settled down.

"For God's sake, Captain," cried passenger Henry Welch, "why don't you turn the boat back, even if you think it is safe? Think of the women and children on board." They were still within sight of shore and hours away from their destination.

But Captain Dority would have none of it. He ordered engines full steam ahead.

By 11:30 PM, disheveled passengers disembarked in Chicago, drenched by lake water, still wearing life preservers, promising they would never sail on the ship again. That day the SS *Eastland* earned the title "the Crank of the Lakes."

Over the years there were other incidents. The most notable was in 1907 when the ship nearly capsized again, this time on Lake Erie. But little was reported in the papers, and the steamship company worked hard to keep it that way. Right up to July 23, 1915, the *Eastland* still experienced stability problems. Twenty miles out into Lake Michigan, the ship reportedly listed to port very suddenly, causing alarm among some passengers. It continued to list for about 200 or 300 feet before righting itself to an even keel. Once the ship corrected, the trip continued without incident, and the *Eastland* arrived safely back to shore on time.

Years later, in court testimony, shipbuilder Sidney Jenks would repeat the words *steady as a church* when describing the ship's launch. He would also admit under oath that "there never was an actual stability test for the *Eastland*" performed.

Steady as a church, and yet the passengers on a fateful day in 1915 never had a prayer.

SUMMER WOULDN'T BE
SUMMER WITHOUT THE PICNIC

———·———

*We have had picnics before, and not one of
them was to be sneezed at, either, but they will
all be forgotten after this one.*
— *Western Electric News*, July 1915

———·———

July 24, 1915, 12:30 AM
In their darkened bedroom, 13-year-old Borghild "Bobbie" Aanstad and her little sister Solveig tossed and
turned, struggling to sleep, knowing they had to be
up early but likely whispering long past their bedtime.
Near Bobbie's bed lay the outfit she had chosen for Saturday's trip to her uncle's employee picnic. It was her
best dress, white cotton with lace trim, tied in back
with a bow, purchased only months earlier for Easter.

A matching wide-brimmed straw hat sat on her dresser. She especially loved that hat, which was covered with delicate flowers. Uncle Olaf had invited his half-sister Marianne and the girls to join him at the Western Electric employee picnic, but it was no ordinary trip to the park.

The girls probably imagined the day. There would be carousels spinning and roller coasters clickety-clacking, the grand parade marching down the main street,

A day at the beach in Michigan City, Indiana.

squealing piglets sliding through outstretched hands in the greased pig competition. Bobbie could hardly wait for the beach and the chance to practice the swimming strokes that neighbor Ernie Carlson had taught her years earlier.

Perhaps they talked about the SS *Eastland*, an immense steamship like nothing they had ever seen before. Sitting on the banks of the Chicago River, the ship waited to sail them away from the city, away from the congestion and noise, across Lake Michigan to the sandy shores of Michigan City, Indiana.

Six miles east, along the Chicago River, 60 tons of coal rattled and rumbled down the metal chute, dumping into the hull of the SS *Eastland*. The boat bobbed and rocked as the weight shifted between two bunkers.

"Fill her up," said Captain Harry Pedersen. With two round-trips carrying passengers back and forth across the lake scheduled for the day, the bins needed to be full, but the captain didn't pay much attention. On one side, 75 tons of coal filled the space; on the other, only 25.

Newly hired chief engineer Joseph Erickson over-saw the operation and afterward assisted the captain in moving the ship into its assigned position along the river, tied up at the Chicago and South Haven wharf. Then he and the captain headed to their bunks to grab some shut-eye before the early morning departure.

Erickson likely noticed someone new sleeping in the crew's quarters. Luman Lobdell was in charge of counting passengers beginning at 6:30 AM, and his boss, Robert McCreary, had made arrangements for Lobdell to sleep on board so he would be ready for the early call. Alongside his bunk sat the counting device he would click as each passenger boarded the ship in a few short hours.

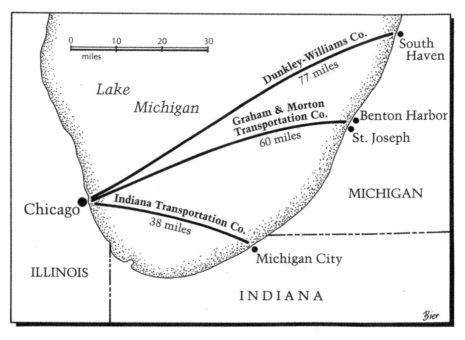

Steamship routes across Lake Michigan.

GENERAL OFFICES

GEO. T. ARNOLD
PRESIDENT

WILLIAM H. HULL
VICE-PRES. & GEN. MANAGER

St. Joseph-Chicago Steamship Co.

WALTER C. STEELE
SEC. & TREAS.

R. W. DAVIS
ASS'T. SEC. & TREAS.

ST. JOSEPH. MICHIGAN

July 16, 1915.

Mr. Harry Pederson, Master,

S.S. "Eastland"

Dear Sir:

Relative to the trip to Michigan City for the Indiana
Transportation Company, you are hereby instructed to make the
necessary arrangements to land head in Friday night, July 23d,
at our Docks. After the passengers have been discharged, you
may proceed with the boat up the river, with the assistance of
the tug, winding at the "Forks" and returning land at the Sibley
Warehouse Docks, laying there over night. Kindly report to Mr.
Greenebaum, General Manager of the Indiana Transportation Company,
early Saturday morning, July 24th.

Upon arrival in Michigan City, kindly report to Mr. A.H.
Leist, who is the agent of the Indiana Transportation Company,
and who is instructed to render you every assistance in facilitatii
the loading and unloading of passengers and who will see that you
are given tug service.

You are to leave Chicago not later than 8:15 A.M. for
Michigan City. You will then immediately return to Chicago, land-
ing at our Docks, leaving Chicago at 2:00 P.M. for St. Joseph on
the regular run. You will leave St. Joseph at 6:00 P.M. going to
Chicago by way of Michigan City, and the boat is scheduled to leav
Michigan City at 7:45 P.M. You will discharge all passengers in
Chicago at our Docks.

Committee in charge of this excursion will be assigned a
stateroom and a place from which they can dispense liquid refresh-
ments gratis. They will also be permitted to sell hats on board
the boat. These matters will be handled by the Purser.

If you are not clear on this subject, kindly ask for
further instructions.

Yours very truly,

Gen. Mgr.

D/E

The captain's orders.

4:30 AM

One by one, lamps lit up darkened windows along neighborhood streets in the town of Hawthorne. Picnic day had finally arrived. Mamie Kelly rose early. She was still settling in to her new life, having arrived in Illinois just the month before. Her husband, Charles, had been transferred from the New York office to Western Electric's massive Hawthorne Works factory.

Because of their recent move, the Kellys hadn't planned to attend the picnic. But excitement for the excursion had bubbled up at the factory, with talk of a tango contest in the dance pavilion and a tub race on the lake. Charles changed his mind, deciding it might be good for the family. Afraid of boats, Mamie didn't like the idea, but their neighbors, the Thyers, convinced her to go. Mrs. Thyer laughed at the idea of any danger. Besides, the families had much in common. Their nine-year-old daughters, Jenny and Helen, would have a grand time together, and so would sons Charlie and Harry. The wives suggested they leave early so that they wouldn't keep the children out too late that night. The party of eight planned to meet at the pier and catch the SS *Eastland*, the first ship out on Saturday morning.

Scurrying to get ready, Mamie placed the overflowing picnic basket by the front door. Charles checked the time and wound his pocket watch. Jenny Kelly sat waiting for her hair to be brushed and tied with ribbons.

"We have to get the 6:00 AM train," said Mamie. "To get to the boat and get good seats." With no time to waste, after a last glimpse in the mirror, adjusting a tie, and checking a hat, the Kellys were off.

5:30 AM

The *Eastland*'s crew tumbled out of their bunks and shuffled to the mess hall, looking for coffee and breakfast. Outside, the thermometer read 70 degrees, and a light wind blew out of the northwest.

From the pier, port agent Martin Flatow looked over the situation, sizing up the ship and its position in the water. He wondered which of the gangways was in the best spot for quickly loading 2,500 passengers. From the looks of it, only one door was suitable. One door aft, near the back of the ship. With the decision made, the crew lugged the 10-foot-long, 4-foot-wide gangplank from inside the ship, stretched it across the water, secured it to the gangway, and attached a chain at the pier end to keep people from boarding early.

As the crew worked, the elevated trains roared along their tracks and streetcars clanged their way into the city. Along jam-packed Water Street, lined with delivery trucks waiting to transport fresh fruits and vegetables to stores across the city, the produce warehouses buzzed with business. In buildings that backed up to the riverfront, workers stacked crates of blueberries and blackberries, and baskets of the first peaches of the season. Frank Blaha rolled out empty barrels from the back of the Waskow Butter Company. The men at Cougle Brothers Poultry piled empty egg crates and wooden chicken coops on the loading dock outside the warehouse doors. Nearby factories puffed hazy smoke into the foggy, smoggy morning air, and tugboats chugged up and down the murky river, right behind those warehouses, whistling their warnings. "Watch out. Make way!"

South Water Street Market, Chicago, Illinois.

Standing: Uncle Olaf Ness, Borghild "Bobbie" Aanstad, and Solveig Aanstad. Seated: Marianne Aanstad.

In neighborhoods surrounding the city, Western Electric workers and their families rose early and loaded hampers with roasted chicken and ham salad sandwiches. They packed mason jars of pickles, along with flaky biscuits and crocks of amber-colored honey. Mothers carefully positioned chocolate cakes and cherry pies on top before closing the picnic basket lids. Fathers gathered up patchwork quilts to spread beneath the willow trees of Washington Park in Michigan City, Indiana.

The cloudy skies soon gave way to a persistent drizzle. But that didn't dampen Bobbie Aanstad's spirits. She and Solveig dashed through their Logan Square neighborhood to catch the streetcar headed down Milwaukee Avenue toward the city. Their mother and uncle followed behind, lugging the picnic gear. Bobbie wore the white cotton dress and tucked her long brown hair beneath the flower-trimmed straw hat. Hand on her head, holding tight to that precious hat, Bobbie dodged puddles and splashed her way to the streetcar stop a few blocks away.

6:00 AM

"I don't want to go, but I must," Helen Greszowiak told her parents. "They want me in the lead of the parade. So I need to be on the first boat out." She grabbed her hat and handbag.

"Don't go," pleaded her mother.

"I must. The foreman said if I didn't go, I would lose my job." So 19-year-old Helen headed out that day, one of many factory girls who had received similar threats from their bosses.

The fifth annual picnic was promoted by a social organization at Western Electric known as the Hawthorne Club. The club organized the excursion and made arrangements with the St. Joseph-Chicago Steamship Company. Prices for tickets in advance were: adults—75 cents, youth—half fare, five and under—free. That sounds cheap today, but most workers earned less than $15 each week. Even though it was a club outing, not technically a Western Electric–sponsored event, management supported the picnic by offering a paid day off to its workers, knowing it was good for employee morale. They also knew it would be good publicity for the company and planned to advertise it in newspapers across the country.

"The moving picture man will take your pictures," promised members of the Hawthorne Club. Women had a chance to be movie actresses in the beauty parade. Twenty-year-old Emma Grossman, a worker in the polishing department, gathered up the paper hat, cane, and paper bell decorated with the words Bell Telephone Company that she purchased for an additional 35 cents. Along with their tickets, female employees were expected to use their own money to buy costumes and props for the parade. Emma reluctantly went, even though she had begged her foreman to be excused. Her sister was being admitted to the hospital the next day for a serious operation and Emma wanted to be there. She even offered to pay for the ticket and not go. But her boss refused, instead giving her a letter instructing employees to meet under their department banner at 11:30 AM in Washington Park. She'd need to catch the *Eastland* if she wanted to get to the parade on time. The cameras would be ready to roll as the parade stepped off—ready to capture the Hawthorne Works's family on holiday. That movie would never be made.

FELLOWSHIP AT WORK AND HOME

——·——

You can buy a good meal anytime for a couple of dollars. What you won't get with it though is Hawthorne good fellowship. That can't be obtained outside of Hawthorne. It is given away lavishly but you can't buy it at any price.
—*Western Electric employee*

——·——

Hawthorne fellowship, pride in work and family, was on full display on picnic day. Most Western Electric employees, accustomed to a six-day workweek, looked forward to a Saturday off and the opportunity to escape the city. Employees generally felt grateful for the jobs they had with a company that continued to grow and value the work they did.

Western Electric Company—Hawthorne Works.

When Western Electric outgrew its Chicago factory in 1902, it expanded just outside the city limits, onto prairie land in the town of Hawthorne, Illinois, where its massive iron gates first opened in 1907. To convey the sheer size of this expansion, Western Electric named it Hawthorne Works. The company hired primarily first- and second-generation immigrants from Eastern Europe, mostly Czech and Polish. By 1913 it was the largest company in Chicago, employing more than 14,000 workers.

Western Electric was the engineering and technology giant of its day. American Telephone and Telegraph, now known as AT&T, hired Western Electric to manufacture and supply products connected to communications. The company made telephones, wires, cables, and switchboards. It produced time clocks and intercoms, and developed the vacuum tube that made long-distance calling a new possibility. Housewives' lives became easier with luxuries like vacuum cleaners, washing machines, toasters, and irons, all manufactured at "the Works."

Until that time, there hadn't been anything quite like the Hawthorne Works, nicknamed the Electrical Capital of America. A huge complex of buildings surrounded by a parklike setting, Hawthorne was a city within a city, supplying every need its workers might have. It had its own railroad—"the biggest little railway in the world"—a power plant, a hospital, and a fire brigade. The company even persuaded the Chicago Public Library to open a branch there.

When it came to social events, the Hawthorne Club planned athletic competitions and dances for singles. Initially a "men only" organization, the club voted to include women in the spring of 1915. Need to learn English or to wire circuits? You could attend Hawthorne University. Want to pursue the arts? Take a dance or photography class. Need dinner or entertainment? Hawthorne had restaurants, a ballpark, and a band shell filled with its own uniformed musicians. With its beauty contests, bowling leagues, and the employee picnic—the biggest annual event—the Hawthorne Club at Western Electric was a social center for workers and their families.

Modern conveniences for your home.

Many "Hawthornites" chose to live within 15 minutes of the factory, and the majority of workers walked to and from work each day. Western Electric even provided low-interest loans so that employees could afford to buy their own homes. When Charles Kelly arrived from the busy New York office, he and Mamie settled a few streets over from Henry Thyer, only blocks from the plant. Small cookie-cutter cottages called bungalows and multifamily two-flats lined the narrow streets, their porches overlooking front yards landscaped with trees and grass. Out back, gardens, chicken coops, and goat pens provided vegetables, eggs, and milk. Many residents built brick ovens in the backyard to bake bread in the summertime and shopped at corner grocery stores that supplied familiar foods from their homelands.

Families clustered together in ethnic neighborhoods, surrounded by friends who shared the same traditions and customs. The Polish prayed together at St. Mary of Czestochowa church, and the Czechs built Sokol auditoriums, large gymnasiums where they could stay fit and strong. A family spirit flourished up and down the blocks, and this sense of fellowship supported the residents, contributing to their tight-knit community.

Western Electric employed an army of young workers. If you were a teen in the early 1900s, chances are you worked instead of attending school. High school was optional, and most families, needing the income earned by sons and daughters, sent their children to the factories instead. Western Electric encouraged employees, especially men, to climb the corporate ladder from office boys to managers. The company took care of the workers' welfare, providing pensions if they were injured or too old to work, and scheduling two-week paid vacations each year.

From the early days, Western Electric employed a large percentage of women, but with an important restriction. Company president Harry Bates Thayer believed female employees should be unmarried. One worker wrote in the *Western Electric News*, "We are in the month of June. The month of sunny days of roses and of brides. A few of us are planning to become brides this month."

But good jobs were important and families counted on the income, so women followed the rules. Much of the work was traditional women's work: braiding, weaving, and sewing. Women's "natural delicacy of touch and carefulness," the company said, made them better suited to perform tasks such as coil winding. In the "twine rooms" they sat on long benches at tables, winding cotton jackets around telephone wires.

When a visitor stopped by the cord-finishing department where Helen Greszowiak worked, he said, "The first impression is that [you have] landed in the middle of a large flower garden filled with beautiful blondes and brunettes picking flowers as fast as their fingers will allow. But in a second [you] realize that the flowers are piles of red, white, blue, green, purple, yellow, and golden cords and that the girls are binding them to soldering clips." The women sat at long tables, gathering and winding the colorful wires before joining them together and attaching plugs.

Women also worked as typists, stenographers, and draftsmen's apprentices. Hawthorne valued these workers, recognizing not only the quality of their work but also the bargain they represented. Women received less pay for their labor, so it made good business sense back then to hire female employees.

A group of Hawthorne women who organized a 1912 suffrage parade demanding women's right to vote became affectionately known within the company as the Window Smashers. This name was originally given to women in England who fiercely protested against the government and in support of equal voting rights. Dressed all in white, with purple Votes for Women sashes pinned across their chests, the group of Hawthorne women proudly marched in the company picnic that summer to express their beliefs. After Illinois women won the right to vote in federal and local elections in 1913, the annual parade continued, but it became more of a beauty competition between factory departments.

The 1914 women's parade earned the praise of Hawthorne's superintendent, Harry Albright. He liked the publicity it brought to his company. Hoping to make the 1915 parade just as memorable, hundreds of Hawthorne women assembled after work, night after night, in the weeks leading up to the picnic. They practiced drills for hours on end to perfect their formations. Some of the marchers resented being forced to practice, but they showed up. That very parade drew Helen Greszowiak, Emma Grossman, and the rest of the young working women to the pier, to the *Eastland*, to make the early morning departure for Washington Park.

GREYHOUND OF
THE LAKES

All dressed up and nowhere to go.

6:20 AM

The picnic was *the* social event of the year for single people employed at the Hawthorne Works—a chance to meet a special someone. Employees Josephine, Mae, and Anna Polivka helped one another lace up tight corsets, slip on white shirtwaist blouses and skirts, and layer petticoats beneath. They were marching in the parade too. Hats crowned upswept hair, and judging from the steady drizzle outside, the parasols meant to shield their faces from the sun would likely become umbrellas.

The girls kissed their mother good-bye. Like every other Saturday, Mrs. Polivka was already in the kitchen, baking bread and strudel for the week. Running late, the sisters rushed down 25th Place to the home of their friends, the Zasteras.

"You girls are late. My girls left a long time ago," said Mrs. Zastera. The Polivkas hurried off to catch the streetcar in hopes of meeting their trio of girlfriends on the boat.

Just two blocks away, woodworker James Novotny and his family prepared for the picnic too. His wife,

Bon voyage, *Eastland.*

The Zastera sisters. From left to right: Marie, Antonie, and Julie.

Agnes, packed their basket, looking forward to the day with her daughter, Mamie, and young son, Willie. Willie was especially proud of the brand-new suit he was wearing that day. He wore brown knee-length pants, called knickers, with a matching jacket. In his pocket he carried a jackknife. Willie's little dog, Carlo, whined at the back door as the Novotnys scrambled out to catch the streetcar.

At his home on Ayers Street, George Goyette dressed in his Sunday suit, adjusting a knotted tie beneath the stiff collar of his starched cotton shirt. As foreman of Western Electric's woodworking division, he knew many in his department would be at the picnic that morning, so he wanted to get there early. Grabbing his straw hat, he tucked a fresh handkerchief into his pocket. Then he turned his attention to 16-year-old

Charlie, an office boy at Western Electric, making sure his son was dressed appropriately.

Long and lanky Herman Krause slipped into the patriotic suit his mother Augusta had sewn for the costume contest. At six feet three, he made a fine-looking Uncle Sam, the perfect symbol for the welcoming parade. The pageant organizers had asked the 22-year-old to play that part, so he left his home with plenty of time to catch the first boat out, the *Eastland*.

Candyman L. D. Gadory packed up all his treats and made his way downtown. He was assigned the job of satisfying the sweet tooth of every child on board the *Eastland*. With a full load of passengers expected, he and his helper, Jimmy Crawley, hurried down to the docks to board before the guests.

Working girls on their way to the picnic joined arms and giggled their way past the eligible young men standing on street corners. They climbed aboard packed trolley cars or rode the elevated trains that spread out from the city like spider legs. As they scurried toward the city, bridges, train tracks, and streets bustled with traffic. It seemed like everyone was on holiday. More than 7,000 ticket holders left row after row of bungalows and two-flats behind, heading east toward the lake and the ships at the downtown wharf.

Bobbie Aanstad spotted twin smokestacks towering above nearby buildings, ready to belch clouds of smoke into the morning haze. She and the rest of the happy picnic-goers, toting baskets and blankets, exited the congested train station and funneled into Clark and Lake Streets. That's when they caught their first glimpse of the ship. The white-painted hull stood in stark contrast with the dark brick warehouses lining the waterway. And across the curving pilothouse wall, the painted wooden letters spelled out E-A-S-T-L-A-N-D. The ship stretched an entire city block in length but was narrow, only 38 feet wide. Tall and narrow.

It stood moored along South Water Street, rocking with the river's current, waiting to transport eager passengers. People oohed and aahed as they approached the ship known as the "Greyhound of the Lakes." The fastest of five ships hired for that day, the *Eastland* had been advertised to complete the ride to Michigan City in less than three hours.

Sitting high in the water, the ship featured four decks above the engine room and storage holds. The main deck, near the waterline, held five gangways on each side of the ship for boarding passengers and loading cargo and fuel. On the cabin deck, also known as tween deck, there were a dining room and an open veranda at the rear. One deck up, the promenade deck held the glass-enclosed ladies' saloon at the front, the popular dance floor with bandstand, and the men's smoking room. A pipe organ, called a calliope, sat at the stern.

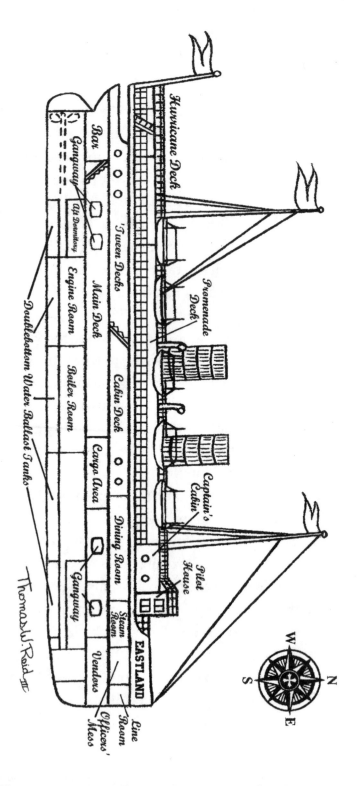

Cross-section of the SS Eastland.

It remained quiet while in port due to city regulations but was ready to whistle out songs like "In the Good Old Summertime" once the ship hit Lake Michigan. The deck featured a walkway that stretched eight feet wide and encircled the ship—a perfect place to stroll, or promenade, in the fresh air. The hurricane deck, one flight up, offered the best views for passengers. High above, it provided the finest observation point, if you didn't mind squeezing into the space not occupied by lifeboats, rafts, and smokestacks.

Captain Pedersen stood in the pilothouse, reviewing charts and maps. He looked out at the morning fog and rain. These conditions might pose problems. Engineer Erickson checked and double-checked all the portholes on the main deck, making sure they were closed and secured. Then he returned to the engine room to oversee the pumping of water to empty the ballast tanks, a ritual always completed before boarding passengers.

The ballast, at the bottom of ships, provided weight and stability, often with heavy materials like iron, lead, or concrete in the base. With a water ballast system, like the *Eastland*'s, lake water could be pumped in and out of tanks to add or remove weight from the hull. If a harbor was exceptionally shallow, the engineer could raise the ship by removing water. When clear of the channel, he could add water to the ballast tanks to make the ship heavier at the bottom and more stable. He could also adjust for a lean, or list. If the ship listed to port, he could order water into the starboard tanks to bring the boat back into balance or on an even keel. The routine of emptying the tanks before sailing meant the engineer would know exactly how much water was being added to each tank. He would measure the amount of water by noting the length of time the valves were left open. There were no meters to gauge precisely how many gallons had been added. Even though he had been in charge of the engine room aboard the *Eastland* for only three months, Erickson was a seasoned sailor and had been an engineer since 1909. He had served on four other vessels with similar systems and knew how to operate them effectively.

Captain Pedersen had failed to tell Erickson that the *Eastland*'s passenger limit had been raised to 2,500. Nearly 300 more people than usual would be aboard that day, and Joseph Erickson knew nothing about that critical change. That information likely would have caused him to adjust the amount of water ballast needed to stabilize the ship.

6:40 AM

"Tickets, please," shouted the man at the gangway door. "Have your tickets ready!" Two federal inspectors, stationed near the entrance, held counters in their hands to get an accurate count of the passengers.

Click. Click. Click. They counted every customer. Precisely. Exactly. After the sinking of the *Titanic* three years before, Congress passed the Seamen's Act of 1915, a series of safety measures to prevent another such tragedy. "Lifeboats for all" became the rule in response to the too few lifeboats aboard the *Titanic*. On July 2, 1915, three additional boats and six rafts were secured to the hurricane deck of the *Eastland*, adding between 8 and 15 tons to an already top-heavy ship. The extra boats allowed the shipping company to comply with the new law and raise the passenger count to 2,500. More paying customers meant greater profit.

With all the new modifications, it wasn't until that morning, July 24, 1915, that the *Eastland* attempted to sail with that many passengers aboard. That's why the inspectors counted so carefully as mobs of people rushed to board and grab the best seats. They didn't want to overload the ship.

Adult male—*click.*

Youth female—*click.*

Adult female carrying baby—*click, click.*

Almost immediately after boarding began, the ship began listing toward the dock. Inspectors had noted in the past that the *Eastland* sometimes behaved like a bicycle when loading or unloading passengers or cargo. A bike wobbles when you first get on and start peddling; then it balances out after you get going. The

Eastland responded the same way. The listing was partially due to the ship's high center of gravity. It was best to have most of the weight on the lower levels, keeping more of the hull beneath the water. As more people boarded and climbed to the higher decks for a better view, the center of gravity shifted higher, causing the ship to lean.

The extra weight of the lifeboats and rafts on the top deck also changed the center of gravity, as did recent renovations to the main and cabin decks. When the wooden flooring had begun to rot and warp, workmen poured two inches of concrete across the dining room floor from wall to wall for 40 feet, and near the gangway doors at the back of the ship. After adding a layer of linoleum to cover the concrete, that extra weight, roughly 50 tons, shifted the center of gravity higher and made the ship top-heavy.

Noticing the steady list to starboard, the engineer ordered his crew to stand by. Erickson, familiar with this type of movement, knew how to correct the problem.

"Boys, steady her up," Erickson called out. The crew opened the valves on the port ballast tank, and for two to three minutes lake water surged into the tanks opposite the lean, below the surface. Erickson was sure the ship would respond shortly.

7:00 AM

The Kelly and Thyer families boarded the *Eastland* and headed straight to the cabin deck, all the way aft, to the back of the ship. While waiting in line to get on, they had spotted the open-air veranda at the stern and grabbed seats on the starboard side, looking down on the dock. Jenny and Helen sat hand in hand, giggling and talking about the day ahead. Little Charlie and Harry ran around nearby. The men discussed business, while Mrs. Thyer once again assured Mrs. Kelly that the ship was safe and there was no danger.

Those waiting in the lines that zigzagged along the wharf gazed upward through the drizzle toward the promenade and hurricane decks. They already overflowed with people, so many people, squeezed close together near the railings, waving and shouting to friends below.

George Goyette waited in one of those lines, wondering if there would still be room for his family by the time they were able to board. He was the proud father of four sons, all of whom worked for the company. There was his oldest, Cornelius, an electrician; Lyle and Frank, toolmaking apprentices; and Charlie. Cornelius wasn't able to join them, but the rest of the Goyette men planned to celebrate the day with family and coworkers. After George's wife, Kate, and their sixth child, George Jr., died in childbirth in 1901,

George left his only daughter with relatives in Vermont and brought his four boys to Chicago to begin a new life. It hadn't been easy, but it had offered the Goyette men a chance at a fresh start.

Once inside the ship, George's son Lyle spotted friends near the baggage room on the main deck. "We're staying here," said Lyle, holding his wife's hand.

The SS *Eastland* awaiting departure.

George nodded. "Frank, Charlie, let's head up a deck. Maybe there's more room up there." When they reached the cabin deck, Frank settled in with some friends near the starboard railing, right above where Lyle was standing. George and Charlie continued their search for seats on the promenade deck. The dock side of the ship was already packed, so they headed to the

river side but had no luck. With nowhere to sit outside, they stepped inside the saloon.

Charlie carried a handbag with towels and bathing suits inside. "Why don't you take that to the cloak room, Son, and check it in? Get it out of the way for the trip," said George.

Charlie nodded and started down the stairs.

"And if we get separated, you and your brothers look me up when we get to Michigan City. We'll all have dinner together."

The Polivka sisters made it to the pier on time and boarded the ship. Once inside, they bumped into Mae's boss, who invited them to join him inside on the main deck. But it was packed, with no seats available. So the girls climbed the stairs to the upper decks, keeping their eyes open for any sign of the Zasteras.

After getting off the streetcar, Bobbie Aanstad and her family made their way to the wide and wet LaSalle Street steps that led down to the pier. Bobbie's Uncle Olaf led the way, pushing through the crowds, keeping a watchful eye on the girls, and finding the end of the line.

"Tickets, please," shouted the man at the gangway door.

Gripping the rope handrail, Bobbie eased herself down the ramp. Marianne and Solveig trailed behind, the gangplank shifting up and down with each step.

When they reached the doorway and had each been counted, they all slipped inside.

Bobbie and her family,
    the Kellys and Thyers,
      the Goyettes,
        Uncle Sam,
          the candyman,
            the working girls,
             the children,

had all raced to catch a ride on the *Eastland*, dodging relentless raindrops that fell from above, descending an unsteady gangplank, looking forward to a day away—a day spent with their Hawthorne friends and neighbors, a day of games and play—never imagining it would be a day that would change their lives forever.

LIKE A PENDULUM SWINGING

———.———

I don't like the feel of it. There are too many people on this boat. —Marianne Aanstad

———.———

7:00 AM

Nurse Helen Repa worked at the Hawthorne Hospital, but not that day. She and two other nurses were scheduled to staff the hospital tent in Michigan City. Her day would be filled with bandaging scraped knees and elbows suffered in the relay races or treating a sprained ankle in the women's softball game. Helen checked herself in the mirror, smoothing her crisp white uniform, admiring her polished white shoes. She remembered to tuck the special armband given to her for the day into her leather bag. The wide piece of cloth, featuring a red cross in the middle, would make her easy to identify. She said good-bye to her mother and her sister Frances and hopped on the trolley headed to the pier. She still had plenty of time to make the 8:00 departure of the SS *Roosevelt.*

Meanwhile onboard the *Eastland*, Bobbie and her family searched for a place to sit on the cabin deck. They wandered about for nearly 10 minutes, past the dark brown mahogany walls in the parlors and through broad wooden pillars that stretched up from the floor, ending in colorful painted scrollwork near the ceiling. Stained-glass panels framed doorways, allowing small amounts of light to spill into the dimly lit space within the hull of the ship. They noticed the grand main staircase, wide with carved spindles and a curving bannister. That stairway was thick with people hunting for empty seats.

After circling around the entire deck, Uncle Olaf spotted four empty folding chairs in a crowded compartment midship, where portholes in the hull provided some light. The family settled there, out of the rain, happy to have found a spot. Once they set sail, they could explore the rest of the ship. Shoving the picnic basket beneath his seat, Olaf huddled with Bobbie, Solveig, and Marianne. The boat listed once again, this time to port.

"I don't like the feel of it," said Marianne.

Bobbie and Uncle Olaf locked eyes with one another.
"There are too many people on this boat," Marianne
said.

She knew a thing or two about ships. She not only
had sailed to America across the Atlantic with two-
year-old Bobbie and her husband in 1902 but also was
the daughter of a Norwegian fisherman and had sailing
in her blood. She understood how a ship should feel,
and the *Eastland* did not feel right to her.

7:05 AM

Passengers streamed down the gangplank, now boarding at a rate of nearly 50 people per minute. Nearly half
of the 2,500 expected to embark were already on board.
The list to port worsened. Down in the engine room,
Joseph Erickson believed that it was probably due to a
shift in passengers on the upper decks. He waited to see
if the ship would correct itself. However, from his location he couldn't see if there were more people on one
side of the ship than on the other.

He decided to start the engines and warm them up
a bit, hoping that it might help to stabilize the ship.
Smoke billowed from the stacks on the hurricane deck,
another signal that the *Eastland* was approaching departure time.

He then addressed the persistent lean by directing
the crew to empty the port tanks. His men followed the

orders, turning the valves several times, sending water surging from the ballast tanks back into the river. In no time the *Eastland* was back on an even keel.

7:10 AM
High above on the promenade deck, the festivities were in high gear. George Goyette stepped onto the outside deck, noticing the time on the large clock atop the

The busy Chicago River.

Reid Murdoch Building across the way. The Rex Quartet practiced their song for the day's competition. "Tip Top Tipperary Mary" rang out across the deck as the singers performed, hoping to win the contest and the $100 prize and silver loving cup. George settled in to the nearby ladies' saloon with his morning newspaper, listening to the four-part harmonies mixed with music from Bradfield's Orchestra on the dance floor. The

five-piece violin and mandolin group entertained the
crowd inside. Young women tapped their toes in time to
the music, hoping for an invitation from a dapper young
man to take a spin around the dance floor. Couples practiced the One-Step and the Turkey Trot, sliding across
the linoleum as the ship gently rocked back and forth.

Preparations for departure continued as the tugboat
Kenosha slid into position at the bow of the ship and
tied up to the pier. An *Eastland* deckhand lowered the
heavy steel towing cable down to the boat where it was
fastened. The tug stood ready to pull the ship down the
narrow river and guide it into Lake Michigan at Captain Pedersen's order.

"We're nearly full," hollered Lobdell at the gangway door. He walked up the gangplank to join his boss,
with only 25 more passengers to go. The crowds kept
pushing forward.

"You can head over to the *Theodore Roosevelt*. Plenty
of room over there," he said.

"How many do we have?" asked McCreary.

"2,475, sir." He continued to click off those waiting
in line.

When he reached 2,495, Lobdell threw his arms out
to either side.

2,496—*click.*

2,497—*click.*

2,498—*click.*

2,499—*click*.

2,500—*click*.

"That is all!"

Several hundred still tried to get on board. McCreary refused the crowds and directed them to the *Roosevelt* and *Petosky*.

"Oh, be a good fellow and let me on," begged one man. "All my people are on there; one more isn't going to hurt."

"If you get on, I will hold that boat and won't let her go out," said McCreary, sending Lobdell back to the ship, turning his attention to the removal of the gangplank, and directing the crew to pull it in.

Laughter, shouting, and music filled the air in anticipation of the lines being cast off. The drizzle intensified to a steady rain, and more passengers squeezed inside and onto the noisy promenade deck. Young mothers corralled their little ones and sought shelter from the showers, heading down to the lower decks where there was more room for the youngsters to run around.

L. D. Gadory had loaded his tray with sweets like lollipops, Cracker Jack, chewing gum, and candy sticks. He and assistant Jimmy Crawley noticed how many of the women and children were heading indoors because of the weather, so they made their way to the main deck, where eager customers waited with pennies to buy candy.

7:15 AM

In the Watson Warehouse diagonally across the river from the *Eastland*, an employee named David Durand looked out from a third-story window. He called to Walter Perry, a coworker.

"Hey, Walter. Come here and take a look," said Durand.

Perry joined him at the window and they both watched, noting how badly the ship was listing to port. In fact, in the minutes they were watching, it seemed to lean even farther to port. They waited for the *Eastland* to level out. They remained at the window and watched.

Erickson estimated that the list had now reached 10 to 15 degrees, so he ordered the valves open to admit water to the starboard side. He personally opened one of them, turning and counting with each turn. "One, two, three, four, five, six, seven, eight, nine, ten." He started timing how long the valves were open, assuring himself that after several minutes enough water had been admitted to fix the problem.

"Someone check the fender strake!" hollered Erickson. "Make sure it isn't hanging on the wharf." The fender strake, a single line of metal plating that acts like a bumper, keeps the hull from scraping the dock. Sometimes the metal could get caught along the top of the pier and keep the ship from balancing out. One of the crew hustled up to the dock to check. Erickson tried to think of anything that could be causing the issue.

"She's clear, sir. She's not hanging up," shouted a crew member.

What else could it be? Was there a blockage in the pipes? Was the valve broken? Why was it taking so long to correct the lean? Were there too many people on the hurricane deck? Back in 1904, when overcrowding on the top deck had almost capsized the *Eastland*, the crew had solved the problem by forcing passengers belowdecks to redistribute the weight. But now, it wasn't only passengers adding weight. The extra lifeboats and life rafts that were installed to make the ship safer were increasing the mass on the top deck.

7:18 AM

In a span of a few minutes, the *Eastland* rolled back to an even keel. Erickson exhaled. "I believe we are getting her," he told the crew.

Harbormaster Adam Weckler watched the ship level out, satisfied that the *Eastland* was ready for departure. He shouted to the bridge.

"Hello, Cap, when you are ready you can have the bridge any time you want it."

Captain Pedersen gave him a nod, eager to get the cruise underway as soon as everything was secured below.

The captain and passengers prepare for departure.

The tugboat *Kenosha*'s Captain O'Meara heard the exchange and began to prepare for departure. He ordered the lines cast off and piloted the tug into the middle of the river, positioning himself immediately off the bow of the *Eastland*.

The crew finished drawing in the gangplank as Western Electric employee E. W. Sladkey arrived late to the pier. He looked at the packed ship and figured he'd head over to the *Roosevelt*, where the crowd was boarding, until he heard familiar voices from the upper decks.

"Sladkey! Sladkey!"

He looked up and saw a group of young men and women from the printing department, where he was the foreman. They waved their arms and gestured. He waved back. The crew was busy securing the gangplank inside the ship.

"C'mon, jump!" they shouted. "Jump!"

Sladkey paused a moment and looked at the distance between ship and shore. Then he jumped over the water and through the gangway door. He stayed on the starboard side and worked his way up to the top hurricane deck at the bow of the ship to meet up with his friends.

With Sladkey's leap, the official passenger count stood at 2,501 with a crew of 70 aboard that day.

STAND BY!
READY FOR DEPARTURE!

———·———

All together, hey! —Eastland *passengers*

———·———

7:20 AM

The rain continued to fall, heavier by the minute. More and more passengers moved indoors. But some hardy folks remained outside, refusing to give up their chance to watch the ship pull away. With the removal of the gangplank, they sensed that it would soon be time for the ship to leave.

At the warehouse window across the way, David Durand continued watching as the *Eastland* once again rolled to port. He observed a swarm of passengers moving up the steep deck, away from the river side, but even that major shift of people did nothing to stabilize the ship. It continued to lean.

Chief Engineer Erickson felt the ship roll again, almost 20 degrees, even farther to port than the last time. That's when he noticed the water. It was flowing onto the deck through a scupper, or draining hold, covering the floor.

"Stop the engines!" he hollered, thinking that they might be part of the problem.

7:22 AM

Captain Pedersen paced near the pilothouse, feeling the recurring list, anxious to get the *Eastland* on its way. He had watched a foolish passenger jump from the wharf after the gangway had been pulled in. With boarding complete, and permission from the harbormaster, he went through his final checklist to prepare for immediate departure.

7:23 AM

The list to port grew heavier, and Erickson directed the assistant engineer, Charles Silvernail, to move passengers on the main deck to help correct the problem.

"Move to the starboard side, please," shouted Silvernail. "Starboard side." Despite the increasing lean, passengers followed directions without any signs of panic. He then spread word to the higher decks to do the same.

Inspector Lobdell, who remained on board to take the passenger count on the return trip, stood near the gangway door on the starboard side. He was finishing a conversation with his boss, who stood on the dock, when he heard a commotion inside.

"The water is coming in! It's coming in!" shouted a young girl on the main deck.

Lobdell stepped up onto the doorsill, stretching to see across the congested main deck, which was overflowing with people. Lake water gushed in through the port gangways across the way. All four gangway doors were wide open, and water poured in through them all. It flowed across the wooden deck, covering shoes and soaking the hems of long white dresses, and down the steps into the engine room.

Engineer Fred Snow saw the amount of water rushing down the stairs toward him. He felt the ever-increasing list. He sounded a warning signal known as the Modoc whistle. *Emergency!* The alarm screeched through the lower levels of the ship.

Woot! Woot! Woot! Emergency! Woot! Woot! Woot!

7:24 AM
Captain Pedersen either didn't hear the alarm or chose to ignore it, instead ringing down to the engine room telegraph.

"Stand by."

The *Kenosha's* Captain O'Meara stood on deck, waiting for orders to pull away. He'd been watching for a signal for more than five minutes. Harbormaster Weckler ran down the pier and shouted a warning to the tug.

"Don't pull on her at all. I am not going to give that fellow the bridge until he straightens up." O'Meara held the tug steady, waiting and watching and hoping the ship would right itself.

But Captain Pedersen didn't hear that warning, still operating on the information that he had received from the harbormaster only minutes before, giving him the OK to leave. He would later admit he wasn't comfortable with the conditions when he rang down to stand by, but he felt things would straighten out once they got started.

Pedersen pressed a button that sounded a buzzer near the back of the ship, signaling stern lines be thrown off. Hearing the sound, a baggage man on the pier responded, casting off the long cables at the back of the ship. Then he headed along the pier, awaiting the signal to release the three forward lines, which were still secured firmly to the dock at the bow. Even though the *Eastland* still leaned dangerously to port, several hundred passengers on the upper decks, who moments ago were waving good-bye to friends on the dock, drifted back toward the river side to get a better view. Now standing 10 to 20 deep in some places, most of the people on the upper decks stood on the port side.

7:25 AM

Again, the ship recovered from the list and righted itself, if only momentarily. Erickson started the bilge pump, meant to remove water from the engine room that had flowed in through the scuppers and gangways. Captain Pedersen walked along the starboard side of the ship, overseeing the lines being cast off the pier. Everything was in motion. There was no turning back.

7:27 AM

"Come on, let's see the boat go out," said 18-year-old Frank Becker to his friend John Stewart as they met near the Clark Street Bridge. The friends watched as the *Eastland* cast off one of the lines. The stern of the ship slowly swung away from the wharf and the bow moved slightly toward the dock. Those gathered on the pier waved good-bye and shouted farewells to the picnic-goers.

"Hurrah for the Western Electric!"

Music mixed with the crowd's cheers, as the orchestra on the promenade deck switched to ragtime music. Dancing had become nearly impossible due to the crowds gathered on the dance floor, so tunes like "Twelfth Street Rag" kept passengers amused, distracting them from the current conditions. It was no easy task for the musicians, digging in their heels to keep from sliding off their chairs and across the floor. Each time the ship rolled back and forth, the crowds made a game of it, laughing and shouting.

"All together, hey!" They slid across the floor, bracing each other to keep from falling. Then they slid the other way. "All together, hey!"

They sensed no danger.

In the saloon, George Goyette heard the chants from the dance floor, but he continued visiting with friends who sat across the way. His chair backed up against the staircase, and he could look through the glass partition that separated the space from the deck. As others tried to squeeze in from the rain, George pulled in a few more folding chairs from outside. With his sons spread throughout the ship, he settled in. Not long after sitting down, his chair started to slide toward his companions across from him. George simply slid it back against the staircase railing and continued to talk with the group about the day and the uncooperative weather.

As the ship rocked, Mrs. Thyer and Mrs. Kelly chatted, watching over their children, likely commenting about the rocking and the way that ships sometimes act. Their husbands sat together, greeting other workers who squeezed into nearby seats. Daughters Jenny and Helen chattered away, sitting side by side and holding hands, excited for the girls' relay race and all the ice cream they could eat.

Down on the jam-packed main deck, the candyman passed out treats as quickly as he could. Tumbling tykes caught his attention, as the ship's motion caused his smallest customers to lose their balance and fall. There were so many mothers and children surrounding him.

A final list to port resumed, the ship rolling to 25 degrees. Passengers on the hurricane deck were again asked to move to the starboard side, but the deck was too slippery from the rain, the angle too great.

The picnic basket beneath Uncle Olaf's chair slid away again. He calmly reached for it, slipped it back in place, and planted his feet in front of it to keep it from moving. With each sway, Bobbie's mother shook her head. Marianne pulled her daughter Solveig's chair a little closer, putting an arm around her shoulder. Twenty-five, then thirty degrees to port.

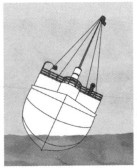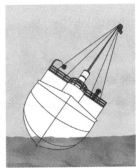

Fifteen, twenty-five, thirty-five degrees.

"This boat is top-heavy," Marianne said. Bobbie grasped the seat of her folding chair and anchored her feet to the floor. She watched her mother's face. Only minutes ago they had rushed down the gangplank, smiling and laughing. What a week it was going to be. First the boat ride and picnic, then her 14th birthday a few days away. She was so anxious for this adventure to begin. But now Bobbie sat still, trying to push away a feeling growing inside her. Was her mother right? Was there something wrong with the ship? She didn't have to wonder for long.

FORTY-FIVE
DEGREES

——— · ———

Western Electric picnic is called off!
　　　　　—Company spokesman

——— · ———

7:28 AM

The ship creaked and moaned, leaning farther and farther toward the river. Thick rope cables stretched from the pier, tight and taut. Thirty-five degrees . . . forty degrees. The floor sloped away from Bobbie, and her chair slipped as she tried to hold on. Eyes wide, she studied her mother's face, trying to understand what was happening. Time stopped. Her chair slid out from beneath her.

Forty-five degrees! But this time, the *Eastland* would not repeat past performances and right itself. Glasses

57

and dishes slipped from shelves and shattered on linoleum floors. The orchestra stopped midnote, as the
piano slid from its platform and careened across the
deck. The refrigerator behind the bar fell over with a
tremendous blast and slammed into the port-side wall,
pinning people beneath it. Beer bottles exploded. Anything not bolted down slammed into anyone and anything in its path. Water continued to pour in port-side
through open gangways and open portholes on the
main deck. Captain Pedersen, racing along the starboard side, realizing the grave situation, hollered down
to the wharf.

"For God's sake, open up your gangways!" But it
was too late.

Benches slid. Picnic baskets, baby carriages, blankets
were tossed into the air. Fancy hats and ladies' parasols tumbled away from their owners. So did babies and
small children. There wasn't even time for passengers
on the upper deck to get out of their chairs. They were
launched from where they sat into the water, along with
anything else not tied down, like ants being brushed
from the table. Terror and panic swept through the
ship. Some passengers and crew jumped through open
gangway doors onto the dock or into the water. Still
others misjudged the distance and struck the side of the
ship as it rolled over, or collided with the wooden poles
sticking up from the pier.

As the band on board the *Roosevelt* played the final notes of "I'm On My Way to Dear Old Dublin Bay," thousands watched in disbelief as the *Eastland*, filled with their fellow workers and friends, rolled over on its side. Policeman Fred Fischer told others, "She just turned over like an egg in the water and made no splash." The SS *Eastland* lay within 15 feet of the steamship pier.

Reporter Harlan E. Babcock had been assigned to the Western Electric picnic story. He had planned to take the *Eastland* that morning but had overslept, arriving right before the capsizing. He witnessed the entire event as it happened. He would later report it this way:

> The upper deck of the *Eastland* was fairly black with people, mostly women and children, it seemed to me from where I stood . . . and in less time than it takes to tell it, in sight of that horror-stricken throng of thousands, the *Eastland*, with its load of precious humanity, many of whom were mothers, with babes in arms and with sweet-faced "kiddies" at their sides, careened, hurling hundreds screaming into the black waters of the river.

7:30 AM

Although the ship turned over rather effortlessly, there was nothing calm about the reaction of those who were trapped or struggling to stay above water. A mass of flailing arms, bobbing heads, and floating possessions spread from the ship in all directions. There were gurgles and screams as parents searched for their children, and working girls grabbed at anything they could use as a float.

The ship plunged, sweeping hundreds of people, including Uncle Sam, into the water. He had been standing near the railing on the starboard side. Herman Krause thrashed about, treading hard to keep his head above water. His red, white, and blue costume starkly contrasted with the muddy river around him.

Onlookers at the dock were stunned. Every passenger struggled—to escape, to breathe, to find loved ones. The *Eastland* settled into the mud, where the water reached only 20 feet deep. The ship lay on its side like a beached whale, half in the water and half out. The letters E-A-S-T could be seen above the waterline, with the rest of the ship's name hidden below the surface.

Before the steamship had fully come to rest, an on-duty policeman at the site called in a "still alarm." His call notified fire companies and police departments throughout the city. Within minutes, patrol wagons and ambulances raced across town, sirens blaring to clear the way.

The SS *Roosevelt*, moored directly in front of the *Eastland*, blew its emergency whistle. *Woot! Woot! Woot!* Crew members directed passengers to throw life preservers into the water, which they readily tossed off the stern of the ship. Other crew members wasted no time in lowering lifeboats to try to save the hundreds of people fighting for their lives below them.

People thrashed about in the water, clustered so thickly that they covered the surface of the river. Some people on shore screamed in terror, while others ran along the docks, trying to help. Some who could swim kicked off their shoes and jumped in to help, or leaned into the river, dragging people to shore. Others offered dry coats or picnic blankets to soaking survivors pulled from the water.

E-A-S-T.

Others, like Otto Blaha, searched for anything that would float. Soon empty chicken coops and egg crates rained down from the loading docks of Waskow Butter Company and Cougle Brothers poultry supply warehouse. Random pieces of wood lying on the piers and barrels that had contained iced poultry just hours before were pitched into the river to help victims stay afloat. Daniel Brazil raced to cut ropes from 15 wagons on Water Street and threw the lifelines into the river. Unfortunately, some of the items meant to save lives ended up hitting potential survivors in the head, and their bodies slipped below the water.

7:40 AM

On a streetcar a few blocks from the river, Helen Repa heard the screams. A policeman galloped up on horseback, stopping traffic.

"Excursion boat upset," he shouted. "Look out for the ambulance!"

Helen knew at once it was one of Western Electric's ships. She grabbed her bag and darted to the front of the car, slipped by the motorman, and jumped off. The passing ambulance had slowed down because of the congestion, and Helen jumped on its back step. She was allowed to ride to the dock because she was in her nurse uniform.

When she arrived at the top of the LaSalle Street stairs that led down to the pier, she wasn't prepared for what she saw. A few in the river were swimming. The rest floundered—choking, sputtering, coughing. Women weighed down by layers of petticoats, skirts, stockings, and laced boots thrashed about. Mothers pushed their children's heads above the water to keep them from swallowing the filthy river water, or worse, sinking to the bottom. Victims reached for anything to keep them afloat—pieces of wood, anything or anyone nearby. They grabbed each other, pulling each other down and screaming. The screaming was the most horrible of all. The wailing and shrieks and sobs and prayers were deafening.

Steamboat whistles called out to nearby vessels in the river and harbor. Almost immediately, anyone with a boat in the area raced to the scene. Fishing boats, dinghies, lifeboats. The men on board the tugboat *Kenosha* sprang into action. With the tug still tied to the *Eastland*, the captain ordered the crew to cast off the line, throwing the tug into reverse and backing it toward the overturned ship.

The boys who had stopped to watch the ship sail away from the bridge saw three girls clinging to one of the empty lifeboats. Frank Becker and John Stewart raced down the narrow steps leading to the pier. Stewart lay across the dock, managing to wedge his shoes into the space between two wooden boards, and held on to Frank Becker's feet to make a human chain. Reaching out as far as he could, Frank gripped the rope attached to the small boat, pulling the three girls to safety.

One of the small boats circling the area spotted patriotic Herman Krause in the water. "Save Uncle Sam!" someone shouted, and he was pulled from the river, still wearing his costume, living to tell his story.

One mother, lucky enough to have reached one of the life preservers that were tossed from the nearby *Roosevelt*, kept her baby afloat upon it and held tightly to her own life vest. She floated and stayed calm, waiting for help.

Candy boy Jimmy Crawley fought to stay afloat in the water. Even though he was small, he held up two women until his strength gave out. Rescuers pulled

Immediately after capsizing.

his lifeless body from the river and rushed him to the doctors, who resuscitated him. "I tried so hard to save 'em," Jimmy said as the color came back to his cheeks, remembering those he couldn't save.

His boss, L. D. Gadory, had been standing in the middle of a crowd of children on the main deck when he realized what was happening to the ship. As the *Eastland* began to roll, he tried to move through the ship and up the stairs. The mob on the main deck surged right along with him, toward the staircase leading up to the cabin deck. There was screaming and hollering and clawing and fighting. The crowd was so thick, it crushed everyone and everything in its path. Gadory fought his way back through the main cabin and toward

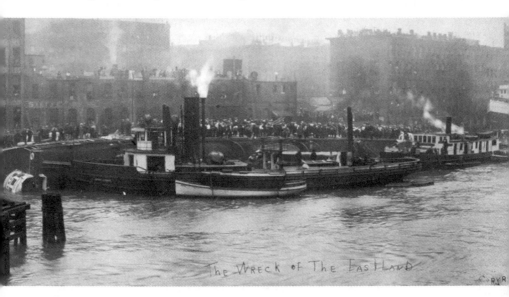

the gangway doors on the starboard side and hung on, shouting to some of the youngsters.

"Hey, get over this way, kids. Come over this way."

Those fortunate enough to have been on the starboard side held on for their lives. As the ship rolled over, they gripped anything they could to keep from falling into the debris that crashed to the port side of the ship below them—a railing, metal brackets along the decks, a cargo doorway. As the *Eastland* landed on its side in the mud, Gadory and others flipped themselves through the door, landing on the hull of the ship as it turned over.

"My God, I wonder what happened to all those kids," said the candyman, shaking his head.

George Goyette's son Lyle and his wife escaped the same way. They were still near the gangway door when they heard someone yell, "Get back!" Pushed to one side as the boat rolled over, Lyle and his wife held on to the baggage room window until the boat settled. He lifted his wife in his arms and escaped through the opening onto the upper side of the ship. Then the two slid down the hull, landing on the propeller shaft that stuck out of the water. They held on to one another and waited. His brother Frank, clinging to the railing one deck above, climbed over the side the same way. He then helped others around him escape the ship. Those survivors found themselves standing or sitting there together moments after the capsizing, on the side of the *Eastland*. They clung to one another, numb, not even wet.

E. W. Sladkey may have been the last passenger to board, but he had no plans to be the last to leave. As the *Eastland* began its final roll into the river, Sladkey, wondering why the crew hadn't warned passengers to abandon ship, gripped the starboard rail. He knew a bit about ships and that his best chance for escape depended on holding tight until the ship settled.

"Over here," he called out to some of his friends, encouraging them to move toward the starboard side. A few followed him, but his shouts were drowned out by a chorus of screams as the *Eastland* flopped over. He climbed over the handrail and found himself on the side of the ship. But instead of standing there and waiting, he noticed the tugboat *Kenosha* backing into position at the bow of the ship. Once again, Sladkey would make a leap, but this time to save his life. With only a few feet of distance between the tug and the ship, he took a chance and jumped, landing with a thud on the deck. Others followed his lead. Unfortunately, only one other member of his party had trailed behind and joined him. That man was the only one of his group that Sladkey saw alive after the accident.

The Polivka sisters were also on one of the upper decks when the ship tipped. They managed to hold on to the side of the boat as it quickly filled with water. Below them, people reached their hands up from the rising river for help. The girls hung on tightly until someone pulled them onto the side of the boat, where they stood with the rest of the crowd waiting.

"Come on girls, we're going to take you off," shouted some men in a rowboat. "Just roll over our arms. We got you." They dropped off the sisters along the side of the river. The girls were in a daze and had no money, but a cab driver picked them up, got them some blankets, and then drove them home. They walked into their house, where they found their mother still doing her Saturday baking in the kitchen.

Mrs. Polivka turned from her work, surprised. She looked from one daughter to the next, wiping her flour-covered hands on her apron, her face blank. "What happened to you?" Their mother hadn't yet heard the news of the *Eastland* tragedy.

Hundreds of daring stories unfolded amid the chaos. In the river, along the dock, inside the ship, people threw their own well-being aside to save others.

Miss Mildred Anderson was one of the heroines. Thrown into the water, she climbed back over the ship's side, took off her coat and hat, and refusing to be helped ashore, assisted two other girls out of the "death cages." These cages were formed by the deck floors . . . that made walls imprisoning passengers in the water. —*Chicago Examiner,* July 25, 1915

Mrs. Anna Johnston, watching at the gate [of the pier] rushed over the side, then before anyone could think to stop her, had rescued seven babies. She remained on the scene until she fainted. Then she was taken home. —*Chicago Examiner,* July 25, 1915

Charles Williams stripped to his underclothes and plunged into the river. First he saved a man who was choking to death. . . . Next he saw a young girl struggling in the middle of the river. Williams grabbed her by the hair, swam to the North Side dock and helped her climb to safety. . . . Then he brought a 3-year-old child to shore. —*Pittsburgh Post-Gazette,* July 25, 1915

Rescue workers crawled up the side of the overturned ship, grabbing hold of shaken survivors who were waiting for help, directing them to safety. Dock workers, crew members, and average citizens pitched in. Captain O'Meara secured the *Kenosha* to the bow of the *Eastland*, turning it into a bridge for hundreds of passengers. Crew members spread a thick layer of ash across the slippery hull to make walking easier. A dreadful procession of families, friends, and strangers followed along the sloping pathway to safety. Dazed. Confused. Sobbing. People wrapped their arms around each other, held hands, and guided one another to dry land.

At the same time, firemen worked frantically to free those within reach inside the ship. Pulling survivors from the open promenade deck or the rear of the cabin deck, they used hands, poles, and rope to create lifelines for passengers treading water or holding on for their lives. Fancy parasols became fishing hooks, catching outstretched arms or the back of a jacket or dress. With no time to lose, the community answered the call.

The Thyer and Kelly families were in an open area at the back of the cabin deck. When the ship turned over, the space around them immediately filled with water and they were swept below. In an instant, Charles Kelly watched his family disappear, sinking beneath the waterline. Chairs, benches, and bodies fell on top of him. He struggled to push them away, eventually surfacing. His wife, Mamie, her worst fears confirmed, fought her way to the surface and eventually emerged from the water.

"Where are the children?" he called out, treading water and searching for their faces.

"I don't know," said Mamie, eyes wide, face tense, scanning the area.

Their daughter floated up, coughing and thrashing about. Charles grabbed her, keeping Jenny above the water. There was no sign of their son. Frantically searching, head swinging one way and then the other, Charles had almost given up on the boy when a small hand emerged from the water. It was Charlie. The Kellys swam over and grabbed an angle iron, a piece of metal jutting out from the side of the ship. Charles called out to those who stood on the hull above him, but nobody responded. The parents tried to soothe their children, assuring them that they were safe and that someone would be there soon to rescue them. "Just hold on tight," they told them, fingers gripping the metal frame. Someone would come soon.

The Thyers were not as fortunate. Helen Thyer and both of her children surfaced, but her husband was nowhere to be found. Mrs. Thyer, a good swimmer, treaded water endlessly, holding her children's heads above the water. With nothing to grab, she used her right hand to hold up Harry and her left hand to grip young Helen. At some point, her left arm weakened, then went numb and began to drop. That's when she lost hold of her daughter. She watched helplessly as

The tugboat *Kenosha*—bridge to safety.

Helen slipped away and sank. Gone. Jenny Kelly and Helen Thyer had been holding hands moments before the ship capsized. Now one girl survived and the other was gone forever.

George Goyette sat near the bow of the ship, the opposite end from the Kellys and Thyers. When the *Eastland* began to go over in earnest, he dropped his newspaper and held tight to the post of the staircase behind him to keep from sliding. And that's when he saw it.

Men, women, and children from the dock side of the saloon and on the deck outside began to be tossed about. George would recall later that it looked "like what you see when you watch a lot of children rolling down the side of a hill. . . . They came slipping and sliding and sprawling down with a mass of lunch boxes, milk bottles, chairs—rubbish of every sort—on top of them. They came down in a floundering screaming mass, and as the boat turned completely over on its side, crashed into the stairs, carrying them away."

All of it came crashing down on George too, carrying him into the water that surged through the ship. He fell against a post that held up the glass partitions across from him, which probably kept him from being swept out into the river. At the last moment he pulled the handkerchief from his pocket and stuffed it in his mouth to keep from swallowing water. Down, down,

down. Pinned beneath the rubble, trapped below the water, George was certain he was going to drown.

Once the crew realized the inevitable, they abandoned their stations, managing to escape by jumping or hanging on to the starboard rail. But Joseph Erickson did one last thing before leaving his post: he turned on the injectors to bring cold water into the boilers. That simple act avoided an explosion that could have made the situation even more catastrophic. Erickson remained at his post in the engine room until the water reached his neck. Then he dragged himself up into an air duct and through a porthole.

People belowdecks were disoriented. The ceiling and floor were now the side walls. The starboard side was above them and the port side below. Where were the escape routes? Pandemonium. Screams. Panic. Survivors emerged from rising waters, sputtering, coughing, and treading water in an attempt to stay alive. There was no escape for those port side on the main or cabin decks. Everything not bolted down had hurtled toward that side of the ship. People were trapped beneath piles of debris, the water growing deeper by the minute. There were many reports of people so panicked that they grabbed at those around them and dragged them under the water with them. Children were separated from their parents. Working girls lost sight of their friends. Most of them witnessed unspeakable horrors as they struggled to stay alive.

Bobbie and her family were trapped on the cabin deck. Within minutes of the ship rolling, Bobbie felt cold, slimy water rise around her. They were confined in a steel compartment, with a porthole on the starboard side that suddenly became a skylight in the hull above them. Bobbie searched for something solid to hold on to, and as the water level grew higher she started treading water, the way her friend Ernie Carlson had taught her. Uncle Olaf reached a life preserver and tossed it to his niece. Eighty-pound Bobbie balanced on it, managing to stay afloat. Her mother climbed up a pile of debris that had settled below the rising river and held on to a piece of the wall with one hand. With her other hand, Marianne grasped Solveig. Bobbie watched her mother. Uncle Olaf turned his attention to those struggling and trapped around them, always mindful of the safety of his family. He kept vigilant watch over everyone around him.

The river water wasn't the only thing rising around Bobbie. Muffled noises sounded from somewhere below her. Odd sounds, like cats meowing and a muted tapping sound. She didn't know what they were at first but soon realized they were the sounds of people screaming and banging on the side of the ship for help. The sheer terror of what was happening must have horrified the 13-year-old, but Bobbie managed to remain relatively calm. That is, until something soft floated over and bumped into her. She looked to see what it was, catching a glimpse of two women, facedown. She turned away and looked up, spotting the porthole high above her. A cloudy beam of daylight pierced the darkness and she could see a tiny bit of the sky. Bobbie kept treading water and made a decision. She would shut out everything else except her family and her skylight of hope.

RESCUE AND RECOVERY

———·———

Gone. Gone. Gone.
        —Dr. Thomas A. Carter, Chicago Health
                                Department

———·———

Nurse Helen Repa caught her breath, then pushed her way through the crowds and climbed up the slippery side of the *Eastland*. She lost her footing and began to fall backward, but someone caught her and boosted her up from behind. When she reached the top, she froze and watched rescuers assist passengers who were hanging on to benches, moldings, railings, or anything else secured to the hull or floor of the ship.

Firemen dragged out survivors whose fancy dresses were no longer white but dirt brown, soaked, and torn. Rescuers observed people with bloodied faces and arms, scratched by frantic fingers trying to grasp at them to keep from sinking below the surface. Many suffered severe cuts and bruises caused by falling debris. Soon Helen snapped out of her initial shock and likely checked in with one of the doctors to find out where to begin. Rescuers laid the injured on the side of the ship or raced them to the nearby docks for treatment. A steady stream of stretchers connected ship to shore.

She followed the procession to the wharf. One doctor examined the body on each stretcher that passed by, working feverishly to find any sign of life. Running his fingers along the side of each person's neck, he searched for a pulse. If he found one, he directed that survivor be given immediate care. If he did not feel anything, he simply uttered the word "Gone."

Helen heard that word again and again.

"Gone."

"Gone."

"Gone."

Doctors and nurses worked on the sidewalks surrounding the disaster. Under canvas street awnings, partially protected from the rain, coatless physicians tried to resuscitate victims who were being brought more rapidly than they could be cared for. Doctors called for more hot water, more blankets, more bandages. Confusion spread in those early hours, as rescuers and responders tried desperately to establish some order. There was no carefully thought-out plan, but an "unconscious harmony among those who sprang to the immediate and obvious task of rescue and first aid" developed.

Helen knelt in puddles, working over those who labored to breathe. "Where are the pulmotors?" she wondered aloud. The breathing machines hadn't arrived, and they provided the only chance for many of those clinging to life. She did her best to administer first aid until the machines came, bandaging wounds, tying off arteries, wrapping survivors in blankets. Doctors assured her that a call had gone out across the city for every available pulmotor to be rushed to the scene of the accident. Survivors who needed more serious attention waited for ambulances to transport them to a hospital.

The other first responders were the priests. Because so many on board the *Eastland* were Catholic, several priests from nearby parishes came to bless the wounded and dead. One priest stood on the side of the steamship beneath an umbrella, a shawl covering his shoulders.

"Ego te absolvo a peccatis tuis, in nomine Patris, et Filli, et Spiritus Sancti. Amen." (I absolve you from all your sins, in the name of the Father and of the Son and of the Holy Ghost. Amen.) He blessed the body of a young girl dressed in white. She wore white pumps on her feet

and silk gloves on her hands. She clasped a gold pocket watch.

"Ah, poor soul," said the priest. "She was holding her sweetheart's watch, perhaps, and they were chatting together when the boat overturned."

Another priest climbed into the ship and began praying with survivors who were trapped in the rubble. Two other priests stood across from one another on the hull, blessing every person carried past on a stretcher by tracing a tiny cross on their forehead.

At the same time, on the side of the ship, Detective Sergeant Stephen Barry and other helpers pried open portholes and dropped long ropes down into flooded compartments. Passengers helped slip the rope loop below the armpits of children and young people, giving a tug when they were ready to be pulled to safety. Rescuers hauled up scores of small survivors, but the holes were too small for adults to fit through; firemen tried in vain to enlarge the openings using sledgehammers and axes. That's when Barry remembered seeing construction workers using torches to dismantle girders at a nearby building site. He flagged down a passing car for a ride, determined to bring back the tools and men needed to open the side of the ship and free the hundreds trapped below who were fighting for their lives.

The crowds near the docks continued to grow as word of the disaster spread. Some came to satisfy their curiosity. Most came looking for loved ones. For blocks and blocks, worried friends and family struggled to reach someone who could give them some answers.

"Where's my wife?"

"Has anyone seen my daughter? She and her friends were supposed to be on board."

The American Red Cross was notified of the accident. This emergency response organization was new to the Chicago area, and the *Eastland* disaster was going to be a major test for it. The organization immediately alerted its nurses to report to the scene and begin lending a hand to the recovery effort.

Police blocked off access to the river as quickly as possible, to make it easier for the first responders to do their jobs. Chaos surrounded the waterfront. Ambulances came and went, and survivors wandered around searching for their lost family members and friends. Bodies of the injured and dead began to pile up.

There was no list of passengers, called a manifest, that would have shown who was actually on the ship. Western Electric employees began collecting the names of survivors and phoning their relatives from one of the waterfront warehouses.

By 8:30 AM, only an hour after the disaster had occurred, the water was cleared of survivors. That didn't mean, however, that it was cleared of bodies. Many were still tangled in debris below the surface or

Holding back the crowds.

held captive within the murky waters of the ship. But those who were thrashing about immediately after capsizing had been rescued through the efforts of others around them.

Someone broke into an empty storefront on Clark Street and turned it into a central information headquarters. Illinois Bell provided a special phone number for the disaster—Franklin 188—and installed twenty phones. Clerks set up an alphabetical system on index cards, with phone numbers, to keep accurate records of the survivors and the dead.

Helen's work slowed down as more and more help arrived. She asked one policeman how many nurses he saw on duty at the nearby hospital. When he replied he'd only seen two, she knew she was needed more there than at the scene of the accident. She hitched a ride to Iroquois Memorial Hospital on a patrol wagon filled with survivors needing more medical attention.

When she arrived, the hospital was in shambles. As more and more people arrived, they sat in the waiting room and hallways, wet and shivering. Not only was the hospital short on help, but also it was out of blankets. Without missing a beat, Helen directed one of the nurses to call Marshall Field's department store, the largest in Chicago.

"Tell them to send over 500 blankets, immediately. And tell them to charge them to Western Electric!" said Helen.

Then Helen called some of the nearby restaurants and asked them to send over hot soup and coffee—whatever they could spare. Next, she turned her attention to the overflow of patients, trying to find a place for the less seriously injured. When a nearby business with an empty boiler room offered to care for them, Helen sent them over, freeing up some space in the hospital. But her work wasn't finished. Once patients were feeling well enough, she walked them to the curb and stopped the first car passing by. No one turned her down. She loaded the patients into the car and told the driver where to drop them off. They'd be better off at home, with families who had been waiting for news about them. Joyous reunions were mixed with sadness for those who would not return.

Once things were working better at the hospital, Helen headed back to the dock. The police had received orders to keep everyone away from the scene, so they stopped Helen. That's when she remembered the arm-band for the picnic. She reached in her bag and slipped the blue-and-white band with the red cross over her sleeve. She had no more trouble getting through the police lines the rest of the day. The crowds continued to build and would reach 20,000 to 30,000 later in the day.

Rescuers faced another difficult situation: how to deal with the rising number of dead bodies. Where would they place the deceased until families could claim them? Within an hour of the disaster, passengers on board the *Roosevelt* had been evacuated and the ship was empty. It was moored directly in front of the *Eastland*, and the first group of bodies was taken there. The *Roosevelt* also acted as a shelter from the rain for survivors.

The struggle inside the *Eastland* continued, and the Kellys hung on, hollering desperately for help. They were trapped in a pit between the cabin and promenade decks. Finally, someone from above reached for the children and hoisted them up to the overturned hull. Mamie struggled, and Charles worried she would faint and slip back below the water. But rescuers managed to pull them both to safety. Charles continued to help drag others out of the hold, but when small rescue

Hospital scene.

boats arrived, two men pulled the children into one boat. Mamie ended up in another.

"Mama! Mama!"

Charles turned, hearing the screams of his children. Jenny and Charlie huddled together, separated from their mother. Their arms reached out, their faces panic-stricken. Charles quickly turned his duties over to another and jumped into the boat with his children. He tried to calm them, telling them they were safe.

When they got to the dock, two police officers lifted Jenny and Charlie from the boat. Charles told the children he would come along as soon as he had found their mother and that the officers would take them to the *Roosevelt*, where they could warm up and wait.

Charles staggered through the crowds, stunned by the sight of so many bodies. This would be no easy task. He stumbled through the noise and commotion, searching for his wife. Soaking wet, and missing his hat, he finally found her in a poultry warehouse, unharmed but shaken. He assured her that they had all made it and returned to the ship to retrieve the children. There was likely a tearful reunion, as Mamie and Charles gathered their children in their arms and huddled in the warehouse basement, safe and sound on dry land. Charles pulled out his pocket watch, wound earlier that morning, to check the time.

7:31—it had stopped as the ship filled with water.

Tap. Tap. Tap. From atop the hull, workers zeroed in on the noise and muffled calls for help from beneath them. The more they heard, the faster they worked. The welders had arrived and fired up their acetylene torches. A shower of sparks shot high into the air. Like blue-flamed can openers, the torches spit bits of steel and cut jagged holes through the hull, creating possible escape routes for those trapped below.

"Here! Stop that! You'll spoil the boat!" shouted Captain Pedersen. He marched into the group of 50 steelworkers who had been called away from work on a new skyscraper to help on the overturned *Eastland*. The men were using their powerful burners to melt holes in the steel hull.

"Who told you to do that?" the captain demanded.

"The police," answered a welder.

"Well, I don't want the boat spoiled. You get off here!" shouted Pedersen.

The crowd surged toward Pedersen, yelling and lunging at the captain, accusing him of causing the disaster. The assistant superintendent of police saw Pedersen.

"Arrest that man and every member of his crew!" shouted the commanding officer. "This damned old tub ought to have been burned before this happened. Spoil the boat!"

The steelworkers flipped down their welder's masks and continued to work as the police took the captain and crew into custody, escorting them to a nearby fireboat for questioning.

"There didn't seem to be the slightest hope of my being able to get out alive. It sounds like a joke to say that I remembered everything wrong that I had ever done in my past life; that is supposed to be a myth that is always told about drowning people. But that is exactly what happened."

Those thoughts floated through George Goyette's mind as he treaded water to keep himself afloat. His leg throbbed with pain. After being dragged underwater and pinned beneath furniture, he held his breath until he was able to push his way from under tables and chairs to the surface. He yanked the handkerchief from his mouth, coughing and gasping for breath. But he was alive.

He looked around to get his bearings, noticing the glass partition that had once been the starboard wall was now overhead. George moved himself toward the "back wall" of the compartment and bumped into what had been the ceiling. He found a cleat sticking out from the life preserver rack and balanced on it to keep himself above the water. That's when he noticed five young women floating near him. He called them over and told them to grab on. They used George as their life preserver, placing their hands on his shoulders, trying to stay calm and save their energy.

The only panic came from a woman who was also clinging to the rack.

"Where's my baby? Where's my baby?" she cried. Her child had slipped from her arms when the ship went over. George shouted to her and tried to calm her, but it did little good. Instead, he turned his attention back to the women around him, trying to remain positive. Perhaps in those minutes George wondered about his own children. Where were his boys? Where was Charlie?

George and the girls waited there for about two hours before anyone reached them. A rescuer stuck an oar through a porthole, and the woman who had lost her child tried to reach it but fell back into the water. George grabbed on to her and tried to calm her as they waited.

The porthole was too small. The only way out was for the rescuers to smash the glass partitions high above those trapped. Shards of broken glass rained down upon them, cutting several of the survivors. George suffered a big gash to one of his thumbs, but it was a small price to pay for escape.

Again and again, rescuers lowered and raised the looped rope, pulling out passengers until only one remained.

"Come on out yourself, George!" yelled someone from above.

George struggled to put the rope over his shoulders and into position, and that was the last thing he remembered until he woke up on the side of the ship with an ambulance surgeon beside him.

George tried to get up, but his right leg wouldn't hold him.

"How do you feel?" the surgeon asked.

"Pretty good," said George, "but I can't walk."

The surgeon snapped George's dislocated knee back into place. Somehow, through all the confusion, his oldest son found him. Cornelius had heard about the accident while at work and rushed to the scene. He accompanied his father to the hospital so that George's leg could be set in a cast. All George really cared about was his family. Where were his boys? Were they all right?

Once the steelworkers' torches did their jobs, the bodies came out faster than anyone had imagined. Sheets of canvas and the remaining coal ash helped create a safer surface on the ship's side so that rescuers could hurry back and forth. Between them they carried stretchers of precious human freight from the overturned ship to those waiting on shore.

"Stretcher!"

Over and over, the call went out and several volunteers rushed in response.

"Gangway! Gangway!" and four men would hurry past with a stiff figure wrapped in blankets. In the crowds and confusion, bodies were laid on the dock, on the bridges, and on the sidewalks. Some of them were already gone, but others battled for their lives. Uninjured passengers walked amid the bodies. Wet and in shock, they wandered up and down the streets, looking for their missing family and friends. Mothers frantically called out for their children. Working girls held on to one another. Men wept.

"Isn't there some building where we can take these people?" Nurse Repa asked a policeman. "Some of them have a fighting chance if we can get them in out of the rain and away from this crowd."

In no time a policeman returned, saying that the Reid Murdoch Building, across the river, was available. The first floor was being readied to treat the injured. The basement—a temporary morgue—would receive the dead bodies.

By early afternoon, the cratered surface of the *Eastland* began giving up those trapped in the inner cabins. Helen was there when rescuers started bringing up the bodies from the hold. They had reached the lower deck, where candyman L. D. Gadory had been working. From there they brought out hundreds of bodies, mostly women and children who had fled the rain-soaked decks to stay dry. All those young mothers. All those little children. Brought up one by one.

Amid the somber work, a cheer went up. A baby, possibly a year old, its little white dress drenched, was taken alive from the hull. With only a small scratch and missing a white stocking and blue boot from one of her feet, she smiled as a fireman carried her to the pier. A moment of joy pierced through hours of grief.

Helen watched briefly and then returned to her work at the Reid Murdoch Building. Fewer and fewer of those brought in required aid. Instead, Helen went about the work of collecting the clothing that had been cut off the victims while they were treated by rescuers. She and other volunteers created a numbered tag and attached it to each victim. Then they labeled envelopes with the same number and placed the victim's personal items inside, hopeful that those details might help identify the body.

A pocket watch.

A set of keys.

A necklace.

A wedding band.

As Helen worked over a man on the warehouse floor, she heard a scream from behind her.

"My God, it's Helen!" Then the woman fainted.

It was her sister Frances, who had received a call at home that Helen was seen climbing up the side of the ship and had slipped and fallen in. Frances thought the worst and came to search the morgue to find her. Helen now bent over her sister, cradling her head, treating her latest patient. A fireman watched the scene and noticed Helen's wet condition. He threw a woman's discarded skirt over the nurse's shoulders to warm her shivering body.

Bobbie and her family remained in the ship, trapped below. Uncle Olaf stayed busy helping others in their compartment. He dove below the surface anytime someone slipped beneath the water. Then he dragged them up and situated them once again. But Olaf always kept one eye on his girls. When the pile of rubble suddenly shifted beneath Marianne and Solveig, and the two sank below the surface, Uncle Olaf was there. He let go of someone else he was helping, responding quickly enough to return his family to a safe place. People fought to hold their grip on anything stable. At times, out of desperation, someone would reach out and grab on to another person, pulling them under. If anyone threatened the family's safety, Olaf was there to protect them.

Time dragged by, and Bobbie treaded and floated, her eyes fixed on her mother's bruised face or the skylight high above. Uncle Olaf continued to help those he could and was eventually credited with saving 27 others. But taking care of Marianne, Solveig, and Bobbie was his main mission. They waited for hours before rescuers reached them and lowered the ropes that would eventually free them. Through the skylight, hope turned to answered prayers for Bobbie and her family. Their nightmare had ended.

Under the glaring lights.

Deep-sea divers, attached to long breathing tubes and "weighed down by lead-soled shoes, helmets, and slugs of lead over a shoulder or around the waist," sank down into 20 feet of muddy water to do their job. It was going to be a long night trying to free the bodies trapped below piles of debris. Electricians installed six high-powered searchlights on the Reid Murdoch Building to illuminate the huge overturned ship. They strung four more floodlights to the other side, shining light down into the dark depths of the Chicago River.

By 4:00 PM, after nearly eight hours of work, Helen Repa stepped away from the scene. There was little more she could do because there was no one left to save. She surveyed herself, looking down at her bloodied and dirty uniform with the armband still in place. The skirt given to her by a policeman still hung over her shoulders. The white shoes she had admired that morning, now caked with mud and tears, carried her a few blocks to the streetcar stop. When it arrived, she pulled herself up the stairs and slid onto the first available wooden bench. With her nurse's bag at her side, she stared out the window at the rain-soaked streets and headed home.

EIGHTY-FIVE
IN EACH ROW

————·————

And down the white plank we went gliding,
precious human freight from the shore.
                                    —Ida O. Anderson

————·————

Later that afternoon, a deputy from the police department confirmed that 600 bodies had been removed, with
more left to be recovered. They were quickly outgrow-
ing the warehouse spaces near the river. City officials
and the Red Cross decided to set up an official morgue at
the Second Regiment Armory, the headquarters for the
Illinois volunteer army. It was large enough for soldiers
to practice their drills and formations, and it would also
be large enough to hold the growing number of bodies expected. A central location for the deceased would

make it easier for families to find their loved ones. So rescuers loaded the bodies from all of the temporary holding places on ambulances, patrol wagons, and delivery trucks loaned from local businesses. Drivers respectfully moved the remains to the massive building on Washington Boulevard, a mile and a half away.

Throughout the drizzly afternoon and night, Red Cross volunteers laid out the bodies in rows of 85, across the cold concrete floor of the armory. They moved among the numbered victims and "with tender hands, composed their features and limbs" to make them appear as peaceful as possible. A patchwork of donated blankets, different colors and patterns, emerged on the floor. A narrow walkway separated each line of bodies. Row after row after row. Bodies were wrapped loosely, with only the feet protruding from beneath the blankets. The families could search for a familiar pair of shoes, saving them the pain of lifting all the blankets in search of a loved one.

A pair of beige canvas heeled boots.

A pair of brown oxfords.

A pair of white tennis shoes.

In a back corner of the morgue, the shoes were different and bundles much smaller.

A pair of black Mary Janes.

A pair of Buster Browns.

A pair of blue baby shoes.

Separated from the columns of adults, the children's section held the saddest remains. Number 396 lay with the other youngsters. Waiting. He would wait the longest of all.

Once word had spread telling where the bodies could be claimed, a crowd assembled outside the armory. Stretching for blocks, they waited for the doors to the bare, redbrick building to open. Many waited to find their loved ones, but the morbidly curious also came, to see for themselves. One woman waited with "dumb horror in [her] wide blue eyes. Her fingers worked at a button hole in her faded red jacket." She pleaded with the guardian at the door.

"It's my baby," she said.

"Not yet, lady, not yet, in a little while maybe," he answered.

"I let her go with a neighbor of mine. She was only three. Won't you let me in now, mister?" she asked.

Workers finished preparing the bodies, while the health department worried about sanitary conditions and the spread of disease by flies. Just before midnight, the coroner addressed the thousands waiting outside.

"In the name of God, I ask you to go away and let those seeking for relatives and friends to come in and identify their dead," said coroner Peter Hoffman.

The signal was given and the doors opened to let in the first 20 families. A sorrowful procession wove through the aisles of dead on the armory floor. "Mothers, sisters, and daughters walked slowly between the lines of dead, hoping and yet not hoping. . . . strong men, hardened to tragedy, broke down and fled weeping from the building, unable to bear up under this greatest tragedy of all." A sob would interrupt the muffled voices. Handkerchiefs covered mouths and dabbed at tears. Sometimes it was too much, and people fainted. There were others who searched up and down each row and still could not find who they were looking for.

The heartbreaking wait.

At some point, volunteers set up a nursery tent outside the building, providing a waiting place for babies and young children. Mothers were told to leave their little ones there to spare them the gruesome sight within. Nurses tended to those who could not endure the pain, offering them a chair, a glass of water, a cool cloth to the forehead.

"Identified!"

The call rose up as each claim was made by a family member.

"Identified!"

Volunteers loaded the body on a stretcher and removed it from its place on the floor. In a curtained-off corner, 50 undertakers and 40 embalmers waited to prepare the bodies to be taken. Clerks from the coroner's office completed paperwork to accompany each one and then notified Western Electric, to keep an accurate list of the dead. A steady stream of people stepped up to a line of temporarily installed telephones. Each lifted the receiver to call home with their sad discovery.

Stamp. Stamp. Stamp. Over and over again, the sound of a rubber stamp hitting a wooden table echoed through the space. *Stamp. Stamp. Stamp.* The ink pressed into the death certificate. The rubber stamp read:

DROWNED, JULY 24, 1915
FROM STEAMER EASTLAND
CHICAGO RIVER AT CLARK STREET

Even though the stamp read DROWNED, hundreds of victims examined showed no signs of water in their lungs. They had been crushed to death in the rush to escape. Regardless of how each died, all victims received the same official cause of death. Officials issued burial permits, and the deceased were transported to funeral homes or released to their families. Volunteers disinfected and dried clothing and other property that had been separated from its owners. They packed it all in boxes and sent it to the city custodian.

Number 396, a boy with dark curly hair, still lay in the back row waiting for someone to recognize him and take him home. Mothers cried over him, wondering what had happened to the boy's family. After thousands walked by, he was still unknown. People at the morgue began to refer to him as "Little Feller."

They streamed in throughout the night and early morning, claiming hundreds. By 2:00 Sunday afternoon, 400 bodies had been identified. The searching continued, but it was slowed down by the large number of people who came just to look. Coroner Hoffman grabbed a megaphone and pleaded with those who weren't there to find their loved ones to please leave so that they could do their work. The warm temperatures caused concerns about the public's health, and officials sprayed the bodies with fly repellant hoping to stop the spread of disease.

"Death's Post Office," as it was called in the newspaper, opened at city hall. People gathered at a little window to reclaim the personal effects of their loved ones. Over $3,000 in jewelry and $1,800 in cash waited to be recovered. A mother found her dead child's toy drum and broke down when she was asked to sign for it. A young man retrieved his father's lapel pin along with his mother's handbag, but his hands shook so much that he couldn't write his name. A half-written letter was taken from the pocket of an unidentified man. It read:

> Dear Mother,
> I am about to take a lake trip and picnic. If by chance I should drown—but oh . . . let's not talk about such things, for you know as well as I that it could not happen on such a big ship like this.

On July 27, 1915, the *Chicago Tribune* posted a list of unclaimed bodies:

UNIDENTIFIED DEAD

At 2:30 o'clock this morning there were seven unidentified bodies in the armory. These, with their tag numbers and descriptions follow:

747—Girl, about 22 years old, dark brown hair, panama hat with black band across top and white flowers, white lace dress, white silk stockings, white pumps, two rings, one set with white stone and other with red stone.

745—Girl, 20 years old, dark brown hair, white waist, yellow skirt, three large bone buttons on front, white gloves, black tie, white stockings and slippers.

53—Woman, 30 years old, 5 feet 5 inches tall, lavender dress, lavender silk hose, black pumps.

396—Boy, 8 years old, 4 feet 6 inches tall, brown hair, full face, broad nose, white suit.

729—Man, 35 years old, 5 feet 9 inches tall, dark brown hair, black shoes and tan hose, sore on left side of face.

679—Girl, 18 years old, brown hair, blue jacket, black corduroy suit, black slippers, black silk hose.

739—Girl, 18 years old, 5 feet tall, grey waist, white silk hose, white tennis slippers, white corduroy skirt.

That morning, the newspapers published stories about "Little Feller," yet no one came forward to claim him. Who was this boy? The coroner transferred the remaining bodies, including "Little Feller," to Sheldon's mortuary. Once the armory was emptied, tarps pulled down, and phones removed, the Department of Health disinfected and fumigated the building.

BURIED
MEMORIES

———·———

What an ocean of tears! What a tidal wave of sorrow and brokenhearted grief.
—Amerikan Kalendár, 1915

———·———

A steady rain continued to fall on the days following the accident. As families gathered to say good-bye to loved ones, the weather matched the grief-stricken mood of the city. One elderly woman, numbed by her pain, raised her open palms to the sky and with little emotion said, "You cry, too." House after house displayed funeral flowers, and the task of burying the dead began. From Monday on, funeral processions became a common scene in Hawthorne neighborhoods. Priests at St. Mary of Czestochowa church performed services for 30 parishioners in a single day. Chicago mayor William Hale Thompson declared Wednesday, July 28, a citywide day of mourning. Businesses, factories, and banks closed, and the flag was ordered to fly at half-mast. That day, more than 500 funerals were scheduled. With the sheer number of deaths, there was a great demand for coffins, undertakers, transportation, churches, and graves.

The grave diggers worked tirelessly. Back then, there were no backhoes. It took two men four hours each to dig a hole. They worked 12-hour days and still couldn't keep up. Think of it. Eight man-hours for each grave, 844 graves. That's nearly 7,000 hours. Some who arrived at the cemetery to bury a family member had to wait as the grave diggers finished the job.

Nearly every block surrounding the Hawthorne Works reported at least one death.

Kolin Avenue, a small street near the factory, was in universal mourning. Every single house had lost one or all of its occupants. A swag of heavy fabric, called a funeral crepe, tied near a house's doorbell let passersby know that someone had died. It was also meant to discourage visitors from ringing the doorbell and disrupting the family. The crepe held meaning too. Black signified an adult, black with white meant a young person had died, and pure white hung in place for each child.

It was customary to hold a visitation at home, so that friends and family could pay their respects. Guests were invited into the front parlor, or living room, to view the body. Extra chairs were brought in and fragrant flowers surrounded the coffins. Florists reported that the market had been cleaned out. Lilies, roses, ferns, gladiolus, and asters. Never had there been such a demand. More than 6,000 wreaths and crosses had been designed and created at a cost of more than $100,000. The task of burying so many had depleted supplies, but floral tributes were all that survivors could provide as they laid their loved ones to rest.

In the parlor of her home on 23rd Place, Helen Thyer knelt and prayed near the caskets, looking down on her husband and daughter lying side by side. She wore a black mourning suit borrowed from a friend. The stream of visitors likely included Charles and Mamie Kelly, along with the rest of the neighbors and workers from the plant.

The Kellys were deeply affected by the loss of their friends, and Charles Kelly wrote this in a letter the day after the disaster:

You might close your eyes and try to imagine the scenes, but you cannot stretch your imagination far enough to cover it as it really was. To be in it is the only way one can realize the enormity of it. . . . Poor Helen and her father were both drowned. The boy and mother were saved. Do you see how close it was for us?

The Polivka sisters walked down the block to the Zastera home. This time when they came to call, their girlfriends were there. Marie, Antonie, and Julie Zastera lay in caskets, side by side, among floral displays in their front room. Mrs. Zastera welcomed the Polivka sisters, likely hugging each of them. "I want nothing but my babies back," she cried. Now the girls were gone, leaving their mother, a younger sister, and a sick father behind.

The entryway to Hawthorne Works, which usually welcomed visitors and employees, was closed. Flowing streamers of black, white, and purple crepe draped the black iron gates, and two large green wreaths hung from the stone pillars that supported them. Condolences, letters that expressed sadness, poured in to the company. Letters arrived from leaders across the country and the world. They also arrived from ordinary people.

To the President,
The Western Electric Company
Chicago, Illinois
  Many hearts are brought down by this regrettable accident. We all hope the dear ones who have so suddenly passed away to their new home are with our Savior Jesus,

who suffered for us all. I am a boy, twelve years of age, and
I regret the loss of your employees very much.
    Yours sincerely,
    Orrin E. Anderson

Without enough hearses to carry them, caskets were placed on any sort of vehicle that could be found. Western Electric lent out all of its trucks. Department stores offered delivery trucks. Open automobiles, delivery trucks, and ice wagons were also used. A dozen caskets were carried to a Polish cemetery in a farm vehicle called a hayrack.

The funeral procession usually began at the home and proceeded through the streets on the way to the neighborhood church. Many processions included a brass marching band playing sad and solemn funeral music, called dirges. Children led the way, carrying large bouquets of lilies and wreaths of flowers. Dressed in their best suits, men served as pallbearers and carried the caskets. They tied a black ribbon around one arm of their jackets or pinned the satin to a lapel. White-garbed girls marched alongside carrying flowers. Many wore a wide black sash at the waist. Clean white dresses, the same type that many had worn to the picnic, soon were drenched with rain and tears and the muddy spray of an occasional hearse or truck passing by. The rain beat down on their bare heads and plastered hair around their somber faces. Families followed behind, and neighbors lined the streets to pay their respects and say their good-byes. Those marching continued on, exhausted and overcome, stopping to pray at church and then resuming their march to the grave.

Survivor Ida O. Anderson wrote a poem to commemorate her fellow employees who lost their lives in the accident:

IN MEMORIAM—PART I
JULY 24, 1915

Eagerly, onward we hurried
A gay, happy, holiday throng,
To catch the first boat was our effort,
While anxiously trudging along.
"'Tis filled: We are going to miss it."
"Oh, no, they'll take on a few more."
And down the white plank we went gliding
Precious, human freight from the shore.
All aboard: Above the gay chatter
We heard the deep ominous call.
For the last mysterious journey
We're aboard,—God pity us all!
A few precious moments we stood there,
Busy talking or clasping a hand,
While smiling someone was speaking
These words: "We will meet when we land."

Burying friends and family.

Some of the funeral processions passed the Haw-thorne Works buildings. Workers crowded near open windows, sobbing and waving good-bye to fellow employees. Just days before, they had practiced march-ing in the employee picnic parade, but this day they marched to cemeteries to bury the victims, most of them under the age of 25.

On Wednesday morning, six firemen arrived at Helen Thyer's home. The Cicero fire chief, a close friend of the Thyers, had arranged for a fire truck "hearse" to transport the bodies of Henry and daughter Helen to the church and cemetery. The firemen served as pall-bearers, lifting the caskets onto the back of the black-and-purple-draped truck. They walked alongside as the procession wound its way through the neighborhood.

That same day, Josephine, Mae, and Anna Polivka carried flowers and followed the Zastera sisters' funeral procession. Their missed opportunity to meet up Saturday morning on the boat meant that one trio of sisters lived and the other threesome died. The Polivkas had planned to walk in a different kind of procession—down the aisle as bridesmaids in Marie Zastera's upcoming wedding. Instead, they followed behind the caskets to Bohemian National Cemetery. In Section 16, where so many other *Eastland* victims were laid to rest, the Polivkas said good-bye to their dear friends.

George Goyette's leg improved, but his broken heart did not. Charlie didn't make it. Late Saturday night, his sons identified their younger brother's body at the morgue and made plans to take him back to Vermont so Charlie could be buried in the family plot. Unable to travel because of his injury, George sent his older sons, Cornelius, Lyle, and Frank, by train to accompany the body. They left the Chicago station Monday afternoon and arrived in Burlington Tuesday evening at 6:40 PM. Early the next day, the official day of mourning, Charlie's

The Zastera sisters—together for eternity.

grandparents, sister May, brothers, and the rest of the family came to say good-bye. After a service at St. Mary's Cathedral, they buried Charlie alongside his mother, Katherine, and baby brother, George Jr. His father must have wished he had never sent his boy down those stairs alone that day. If only he had kept Charlie nearby. George Goyette saved so many young people around him that day. Surely he could have saved his own son.

There is no record of how Bobbie Aanstad spent Wednesday, but July 28 was her 14th birthday. She likely celebrated quietly at home. What had started out as a wonderful beginning to her birthday week turned into a horrific event that she would never be able to forget. She and her family must have felt grateful to have survived.

By Friday, more than five days after the disaster, "Little Feller" remained unclaimed. "The little chap struck at the heart strings of the entire city." Fifteen-year-old May Taylor sent a letter to the morgue with 15 cents inside. She asked that it be used to buy flowers for the boy. Policeman George Friend opened the envelope, and after reading the request, added another dollar. People sent dozens of wreaths and bouquets of roses. They pleaded to pay for the services to finally put this boy to rest. The Boy Scouts started planning and raised enough money to give him a scout hero's funeral with an honor guard. They would escort Comrade 396 to his final resting place.

Meanwhile, three playmates wondered what had happened to their friend Willie. They hadn't seen him for days. Then one of them heard about "Little Feller."

After reading the article describing a lonely little body wearing a brown suit and carrying a jackknife, they thought it might be Willie. Alice and Walter Cech, and their friend Frank Rezabeck, headed to Sheldon's funeral home and "braved the horrors of the [place] and immediately they set eyes upon the ashen face of the little feller and called him by name, just as if they expected him to answer."

"That's him—Willie!" said Frank Rezabeck. He reached down and touched his pal with a grimy hand. "Yep, I know it's him. 'Member Walt, how we was wishin' we could go along?" said Frank.

Willie's own uncle, who had come from another city, wasn't sure it was his nephew.

"We been livin' right next door to him," said Frank. "We was at his birthday party when he turned 7. We used to go to school together and play together ev'ry day. Get Willie's grandma—she's all that's left of 'em next door. She'll tell you."

The police sent an automobile to bring Willie's grandmother to the funeral home. Mrs. Agnes Martenek walked into the room that overflowed with floral arrangements, carrying a small package in her hands. She had been crying.

"If it's Willie, he's got on pants like these," she said. She unwrapped the parcel and handed the policeman a pair of brown knickerbockers. "It was a new suit he went to the picnic in, and two pairs of pants came with it. These are the others."

Sure enough, the pants matched. Willie's grandma, his Babička, looked at her grandson, who had been missing for almost a week, then sat down by his side and wept.

Why had it taken so long? Where were the rest of his family members? They were all gone. His father, mother, and sister had all died that day too. There was no one left to claim number 396. But now he had a name. He was Willie Novotny, and his grandmother had finally come to take him home.

That night, Willie's body lay beside his parents and sister. Friends and neighbors filed by to pay their final respects to James, Agnes, Mamie, and Willie. Willie's little dog Carlo "stood outside the death room whining as he sensed the tragedy that had taken away his little master."

The city held a grand funeral for Willie and his family, as elaborate as any the city had ever held. More than 5,000 people turned out and lined the streets outside the Bohemian School, where Willie was a student. The building was draped in black-and-white crepe, and floral arrangements and wreaths surrounded the coffins of the family. Members of the mounted police, a 25-piece marching band, four companies of Boy Scouts, and hundreds of schoolchildren came to say good-bye to Willie Novotny. A drumroll echoed through the street and a Boy Scout stepped forward and played "Taps." There were speeches too.

"Chicago wants not revenge, but justice. This city will rise up in her might and demand that this sacrifice of life be not in vain. The 'little feller' is dead, but out of his death will be born a new sense of responsibility for public safety." Mayor Thompson said that Willie represented all the victims of the *Eastland* disaster, and that the ceremony was a way to honor each and every one.

A vocal chorus sang the Czech national anthem, "Kde Domov Muj" (Where Is My Home?).

Where Is My Home?
Where is my home, where is my home?
Water roars across the meadows,
Pinewoods rustle among rocks,
The orchard is glorious with spring blossom,
Paradise on earth it is to see.
And this is that beautiful land,
The Czech land, my home,
The Czech land, my home!

When it was time to leave, Boy Scouts carried their little friend's white coffin, draped in an American flag, and loaded it into a hearse. The undertaker led the way to Bohemian National Cemetery.

Bohemian National Cemetery.

The entrance came into view. It was like a Czech castle, cream-colored limestone walls with a red tile roof. Twin turrets framed the arched entry and the bell in the tower tolled into the misty air. And waiting there on either side of the opened iron gates were 100 children from the Bohemian orphanage. Dressed all in white, the orphans welcomed Willie Novotny and his family to their final home.

The procession made its way along the narrow, winding roads of the cemetery—roads that wound through sections filled with nearly 150 freshly dug graves. Brown dirt mounds still dotted the wet, green grass. Days earlier, other families had huddled over the tombs of their loved ones, tossing flowers on caskets being lowered into the earth. Willie's procession continued, bearing to the right, ending at Section Four. There, at the far end of a long row, the Novotny family was laid to rest next to a younger sister already in the ground. The headstone being engraved would read: HERE RESTS IN THE LORD— THE NOVOTNY FAMILY—WHO DIED JULY 24, 1915—EASTLAND DISASTER.

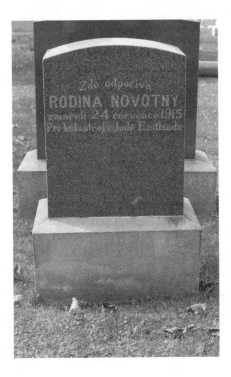

The Novotny grave.

That day, Willie Novotny represented all those inno-
cent people who set out for a joyful day with family and
friends, whose lives would never be the same. The victims of the SS *Eastland* were buried that rainy July 1915,
most in cemeteries across the city of Chicago. They still
lie in graves next to sisters and brothers, mothers and
fathers.

EPILOGUE

—— · ——

Within hours of the *Eastland*'s capsizing, a coroner's jury began investigating the cause of the accident. The public demanded answers, and the search for truth began immediately after the tragedy. Coroner Peter Hoffman's job was to investigate any unexpected, violent, or suspicious deaths in the city. While he focused much of his time on how to handle the growing number of bodies, he also assembled a group of six men to serve as jurors responsible for weighing the evidence. Why had the *Eastland* "turned turtle" in the Chicago River within 20 feet of the wharf? Who was to blame? Captain Pedersen? Chief Engineer Erickson? The ship owners? Did Western Electric bear any responsibility?

From July 24 to July 29, witnesses testified about how many people boarded, where the crowds seemed to gather, what steps the engineer took to balance out the ship, and what orders were given by the captain. They interviewed marine experts and past captains of the ship. The coroner demanded information about modifications to the ship and other incidents of near capsizing that had occurred over the years. The jury learned that while Western Electric employees were involved in the excursion, the company could not be held responsible because the picnic was sponsored by the Hawthorne Club. Western Electric was off the hook.

The coroner and the jury visited the scene and stood on the overturned hull of the *Eastland*, which still rested in the muddy river. They peered deep inside to find evidence that might help them understand what had happened. They examined life jackets, portholes, and the jagged openings cut into the steel walls. After all the evidence had been considered, the headline on July 29, 1915, read:

Six Are Held on Manslaughter

Captain Pedersen, Chief Engineer Erickson, and four officers of the St. Joseph-Chicago Steamship Company, owners of the *Eastland*, were charged.

It was the first investigation held to examine the evidence. A federal grand jury followed, lasting two months. The charge of manslaughter, killing another person without intent, was changed to "conspiracy to operate an unsafe ship." Almost immediately, those accused were arrested, and a criminal trial was begun in Grand Rapids, Michigan. A team of lawyers assembled to defend the men, but an up-and-coming attorney named Clarence Darrow represented Joseph Erickson. Darrow would eventually become one of the most well-known trial lawyers of his time.

Shipbuilder Sidney Jenks received a summons to appear in court for the trial. He walked into the courtroom, bringing along an eight-foot wooden model of the *Eastland*, to better explain the ship's features and answer questions regarding the possible cause of the accident.

"When the *Eastland* was built," said Jenks, "she was designed to be the fastest boat on Lake Michigan. I wanted her to have a speed of 20 miles an hour in order to rush perishable fruit from . . . Michigan points to the Chicago markets. At that time, she was not intended to carry more than 500 passengers."

Darrow asked Jenks if he ever worried about the fact that the *Eastland* had been changed into an excursion boat and that it had a 2,500-passenger capacity.

"I had no way of knowing the quantity of its business after it left our yards," said Jenks. "No, I didn't worry about the *Eastland*."

Darrow also asked if Jenks thought the *Eastland* was a safe boat.

"I considered the *Eastland* the strongest boat of her kind on the lakes and did not regard her as a 'cranky' boat." Jenks explained that the ship he originally designed and built was safe, but he also admitted that there was no stability test. He did recall the launch of the ship on that warm spring day in 1903.

"The boat slid into the water on its side at the launching," he said. "And when it dropped into the water, it tilted in the opposite direction to an angle of 45 degrees, then righted itself as straight as a church, satisfactorily demonstrating its stability."

In the end, despite all the testimony and questions about safety, overloading, coal bunkers, captain's orders, engineer's responses, and modifications, the ruling handed down in the criminal trial declared that those involved did not work together to cause the accident.

Nearly 20 years after the disaster, a civil trial began. A civil trial examines evidence to see if anyone is financially responsible for damages. If those charged were found guilty, the insurance company would have had to pay each of the 844 victims $10,000. If they were found innocent, the families would receive nothing. The trial lasted for months, but when the results came in December 1933, the court ruled that the SS *Eastland* was seaworthy and that the management had no reason to believe it was unsafe to operate. In the end, Joseph Erickson was blamed for improper operation of the ballast tanks. But the engineer, the "fall guy" of the *Eastland* disaster, had died of heart disease in 1919. No one else was held responsible for all those deaths.

Following the disaster, the SS *Eastland* was sold to the US Navy and refitted as a gunboat. It was renamed the USS *Wilmette* and was used as a training ship for sailors for nearly 30 years. Before placing it into the fleet, the navy fixed the ballast system. However, because of the ship's history of being "cranky," the *Wilmette* never operated without full tanks. The red and rusty ballast tanks, kept full over the years, ensured no further incidents on board. The ship remained in service until after World War II. The *Eastland*—Greyhound of the Lakes—would never again sail as a pleasure craft on the Great Lakes.

LIFE AFTER THE EASTLAND DISASTER

Borghild "Bobbie" Aanstad—Bobbie was known for being a happy, spunky, outgoing girl. The *Eastland* disaster didn't change that. Her love of the water continued too. She grew up, married, and raised a family. After her first husband died, she reconnected with Ernie Carlson, the neighbor who had taught her how to swim years earlier, and they married. Bobbie's granddaughters and grandson-in-law went on to establish the

Eastland Disaster Historical Society to honor her and to remember the 844. She died in 1991 at the age of 90.

Thyer family—Helen and her son Harry continued to live on 23rd Place following the disaster. Helen never remarried after losing her husband and daughter. Harry eventually went to work at the Hawthorne plant. According to his grandson, the company had an unofficial policy of hiring survivors of the *Eastland*. Years later, Harry started his own family and shared a home with Helen, just a mile away from where he grew up. Helen died in 1957 at the age of 79.

The SS *Eastland* raised from the Chicago River.

George Goyette family—George and his three surviving sons remained in Chicago. George continued as a foreman at Western Electric and eventually remarried after being widowed for nearly 20 years. He died at the age of 67. George's body made the trip back to Burlington, Vermont, where he was buried in the family plot near his first wife and beloved son Charlie.

Polivka and Zastera sisters—The Polivka girls returned to work at Western Electric. We don't know what happened to the Zastera family after losing their three daughters. They had relied on the girls' income to

support a mother, invalid father, and younger sister. The family probably received about $1,600 from the Red Cross following the deaths. All the Zasteras are buried together at Bohemian National Cemetery.

Helen Repa—Helen returned to her work as a nurse at Western Electric. At age 36, she married Frank Tomek and later had a son. By 1930, according to census data, Helen no longer worked as a nurse.

Captain Harry Pedersen—After the *Eastland* disaster, Captain Pedersen returned to his hometown of Millburg, Michigan, never to command another ship. He and his wife led a quiet life there until he died on July 25, 1939—one day after the 24th anniversary of the event.

Chief Engineer Joseph Erickson—Joseph served as a lieutenant in World War I. He returned from Europe after developing a heart condition. He died at home in Grand Haven, Michigan, at the age of 37. The man who risked his life to stop the engines and prevent an explosion was found guilty of criminal negligence, even though he was already dead. He was the only man ever charged in the accident.

AUTHOR'S NOTE

——— · ———

When I was five years old, my family and I climbed aboard the steamship SS *Canadiana* in Toledo, Ohio. The ship was built in 1910 and was similar to the *Eastland.* We were headed for a day of picnics and play at an amusement park across Lake Erie. I remember looking out from open decks and listening to the band play. My siblings and I chased each other across the dance floor and in between decks. I wore my souvenir sailor's cap on my head and waited at the candy counter with nickels and dimes. I had never seen a ship that size before.

I imagine the people who boarded the *Eastland* 55 years earlier might have felt the way I did. Could any have dreamt they'd be part of this famous maritime disaster? I first found out about the *Eastland* when I was teaching Illinois history to fourth and fifth graders. As I read about it, I kept wondering, *How did something this tragic happen? Why don't I know more about this?* Maybe you've wondered that too.

I read everything I could find on the topic. Like a detective with an incredible mystery to solve, I took notes and printed out articles from newspapers, filing them in binders. In the *Western Electric News*, I read the stories of George Goyette, the Kellys, the Thyers, and Helen Repa. When I learned about Bobbie Aanstad's family story, I knew I wanted to tell the *Eastland*'s tragedy through the eyes of the people who witnessed it.

One question haunted me throughout my research: Why had this story been buried for so long? Most people know about the *Titanic* but not the *Eastland*. Here are a few reasons why it may be missing from our collective memory.

⚓ World War I was on everyone's mind, and even though the United States wouldn't enter the war for almost two more years, people worried. Within a week of the disaster, the front-page news of the *Eastland* incident had been replaced with war coverage.

⚓ In those days, when people were upset about bad news, they often chose not to talk about it. They believed it was better not to mention the bad thing. Mothers warned their children to remain silent and not ask questions. If you didn't talk about it, it would go away. The trauma caused people to bury their stories.

↳ The victims were poor, working-class immigrants and their families. There were no rich and famous celebrities on board, like on *Titanic*. Ninety percent of the victims were women and children. They were someone's wife or daughter or sister. They were someone's baby or little girl or boy. Seventy percent of the victims were under the age of 25.

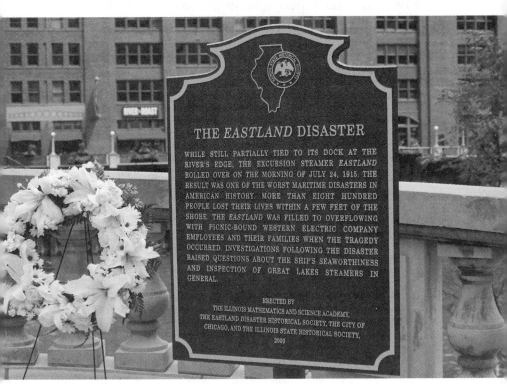

The *Eastland* disaster memorial plaque.

It's good for us to remember the bravery of those
who endured; people like Bobbie, George, and Helen.
It's also important to keep in mind all those who didn't
survive, like Charlie, the Zasteras, and Willie Novotny.
Sometimes, grand monuments or museums are built
to commemorate an important historical event. Other
times, small plaques, like the SS *Eastland* memorial,
which sits at the corner of Wacker Drive and LaSalle
Street in Chicago, can remind us of the past. But we can
also keep those buried memories alive by sharing the
stories of ordinary people—regular folks out to enjoy
a day with their Hawthorne friends and neighbors, a
day of games and picnics and play. This book helps us
remember the 844 people who lost their lives on the
banks of the Chicago River on July 24, 1915. These
words honor their memory.

ACKNOWLEDGMENTS

——·——

I wish to thank Ted and Barbara Wachholz of the East-land Disaster Historical Society for their willingness to support my journey and for sharing the stories of the 844. Thank you to my former students, who gave me the chance to practice writing each day in our class-room. I am indebted to Hamline University's MFAC program, especially to author Claire Rudolf Murphy, who guided me and challenged me to make my words "sparkle." Thank you to editor Lisa Reardon at Chicago Review Press, for giving me my first opportunity to be published. Thanks also to Ellen Hornor for holding my hand through the revision process and to Sarah Olson for her beautiful design work. And to my family and friends, especially Dan, Lindsay, and Andrew, who believed in me before I believed in myself—I am filled with gratitude.

NOTES

—— · ——

A NOTE ON DIALOGUE

It's impossible to interview eyewitnesses when an event occurred over 100 years ago. But that doesn't mean that nonfiction writers can make up what people said. Dialogue must be based on reliable sources. Whenever I included quoted conversation spoken by the main characters in *Capsized!* I based it on newspaper reports, magazine articles, court testimony, or stories from the *Western Electric News*. There are a few bits of dialogue, like "Tickets, please!" or "Watch out! Make way!" that I imagined would have been spoken during the incident. All other dialogue is based on valid sources, and those notes can be found below. If I could not find evidence that an individual said the words, I did not include them in the book.

PROLOGUE

"struck a beribboned bottle of": Dorothy Marie Mitts, *That Noble Country: The Romance of the St. Clair River Region* (Philadelphia: Dorrance, 1968), 133.

"She came right back up": George Woodman Hilton, *Eastland: Legacy of the Titanic* (Stanford, CA: Stanford University Press, 1995), 31.

"Engines in check!": Hilton, *Eastland*, 46.

"The list will grow no worse": Hilton, *Eastland*, 47.

"the passengers refused to obey": "Scare Onboard a Steamer," *Chicago Daily Tribune*, July 18, 1904.

"For God's sake, Captain, why": Transcript of Testimony: Before the Coroner's Jury, July 24, 25, 26, 27, 28, 29, on the Body of Kate Austin and All Others Lost by the Overturning of the Excursion Steamer Eastland While Tied to the Dock at Clark and S. Water Streets in the City of Chicago, 116 (1915) (testimony of Mr. Maclay Hoyne).

"the Crank of the Lakes": R. W. Hicks, "The Eastland Disaster," *Safety Engineering: Prevention of Needless Waste by Fires and Accidents* 30 (July–December 1915): 103.

200 or 300 feet: Ted Wachholz, *The Eastland Disaster* (Charleston, SC: Arcadia, 2005), 123.

"there never was an actual": "Eastland Never Tested," *New York Times*, January 23, 1916.

CHAPTER 1: SUMMER WOULDN'T BE SUMMER WITHOUT THE PICNIC

"Fill her up": Hilton, *Eastland*, 90.

laughed at the idea of: C. C. Kelly, "What the Survivors Tell," *Western Electric News*, August 1915.

"We have to make the 6:00 AM train": "The History: The Eastland Disaster," Eastland Disaster Historical Society, www.eastland disaster.org/history/eastland-disaster.

"I don't want to go": "Responsibility of Western Electric in Eastland Horror," *Chicago Day Book*, July 26, 1915.

"The moving picture man will": F.S., "Forced to Buy Tickets," *Chicago Day Book*, July 29, 1915.

paper hat, cane, and paper bell: "Responsibility of Western Electric in Eastland Horror," *Chicago Day Book*, July 26, 1915.

CHAPTER 2: FELLOWSHIP AT WORK AND HOME

first- or second-generation immigrants: Wachholz, *Eastland Disaster*, 25.

"the biggest little railway": Austin Weber, "The Hawthorne Works," *Assembly Magazine*, August 1, 2002, www.assemblymag.com /articles/88188-the-hawthorne-works.

female employees should be unmarried: Stephen B. Adams and Orville R. Butler, *Manufacturing the Future: A History of Western Electric* (Cambridge: Cambridge University Press, 1999), 103.

"We are in the month": A.H., "Vacation Thoughts and Suggestions," *Western Electric News*, June 1913.

"natural delicacy of touch": Wachholz, *Eastland Disaster*, 26.

"The first impression is that": Lillian M. Wendemuth, "Our Women and Their Work," *Western Electric News*, April 1913.

Window Smashers: "A Date Never to be Forgotten," *Western Electric News*, April 1913.

CHAPTER 3: GREYHOUND OF THE LAKES

"You girls are late": "The 844: Polivka Sisters Become Pall Bearers," Eastland Disaster Historical Society, July 8, 2015, www .eastlanddisaster.org/news/the-844-polivka-sisters-became -pall-bearers-for-friends.

between 8 and 15 tons: Hilton, *Eastland*, 82.

behaved like a bicycle: Hilton, *Eastland*, 44.

two inches of concrete across: Hilton, *Eastland*, 71.

"Boys, steady her up": Hilton, *Eastland*, 96.

"Why don't you take that": George A. Goyette, "What the Survivors Tell," *Western Electric News*, August 1915.

CHAPTER 4: LIKE A PENDULUM SWINGING

"I don't like the feel": Barbara and Ted Wachholz, interview by author, March 4, 2016.

nearly 50 people per minute: *Investigation of Accident to the Steamer "Eastland": Chicago Ill., July 24 to August 5, 1915, Printed for the use of the Committee on Merchant Marine and Fisheries*, 64th Congress, 33 (1916) (testimony of Luman Lobdell).

"If you get on, I": *Investigation of Accident*, 19 (testimony of Robert H. McCreary).

He called to Walter Perry: Hilton, *Eastland*, 100.
"Someone check the fender strake!": Hilton, *Eastland*, 102.
"I believe we are getting": *Before the Coroner's Jury*, 115 (testimony of Fred Snow).
"Hello, Cap, when you are": Hilton, *Eastland*, 102.
Sladkey's leap: Hilton, *Eastland*, 103.

CHAPTER 5: STAND BY! READY FOR DEPARTURE!

"Stop the engines!": Hilton, *Eastland*, 104.
"The water is coming in!": *Investigation of Accident*, 31 (testimony of Luman Lobdell).
a warning signal known as: Hilton, *Eastland*, 105.
"Stand by": Hilton, *Eastland*, 106.
"Don't pull on her at": Michael McCarthy, *Ashes Under Water: The SS Eastland and the Shipwreck That Shook America* (Guilford, CT: Lyons, 2014), 109.
"Come on, let's see the": "Human Chain Saves Three," *Pittsburgh Post-Gazette*, July 25, 1915.
"Hurrah for the Western Electric!": "Human Chain Saves Three," *Pittsburgh Post-Gazette*, July 25, 1915.
"All together, hey!": Hilton, *Eastland*, 109.

CHAPTER 6: FORTY-FIVE DEGREES

"For God's sake, open up": Hilton, *Eastland*, 109.
like ants being brushed from: Harlan E. Babcock, "Harley Babcock Escaped Eastland—Tells How," *Republican-Northwestern* (Belvedere, IL), July 27, 1915.
rolled over on its side: Hilton, *Eastland*, 109.
"She just turned over like an": Hilton, *Eastland*, 109.
"The upper deck of the": Babcock, "Harley Babcock Escaped."
clustered so thickly that they: Helen Repa, "The Experiences of a Hawthorne Nurse," *Western Electric News*, August 1915.
"Excursion boat upset": Repa, "Experiences of a Hawthorne Nurse."
the screaming was the most: Repa, "Experiences of a Hawthorne Nurse."

three girls clinging to the: "Human Chain Saves Three," *Pittsburgh Post-Gazette,* July 25, 1915.

"I tried so hard to": "Panic on Boat Indescribable," *Washington Times,* July 24, 1915.

"Hey, get over this way": Wilbur Cross, "Disaster at the Dock," *Coronet,* September 1957, 136.

"My God, I wonder what": Cross, "Disaster at the Dock," 136.

"Get back!": "Drowned in Chicago Disaster," *Burlington (VT) Weekly Free Press,* July 29, 1915.

"Come on girls, we're going": Josephine (Polivka) Engenhart, "Survivor Story: Polivka Sisters," Eastland Disaster Historical Society, September 28, 2015, www.eastlanddisaster.org/news/survivor-story-polivka-sisters.

"What happened to you?": Engenhart, "Survivor Story."

"Where are the children?": Kelly, "What the Survivors Tell."

When the Eastland *began to:* Goyette, "What the Survivors Tell."

"like what you see when": Goyette, "What the Survivors Tell."

turn on the injectors to: Hilton, *Eastland,* 111.

two women, facedown: Wachholz interview, March 4, 2016.

CHAPTER 7: RESCUE AND RECOVERY

"Gone": Hilton, *Eastland,* 114.

partially protected from the rain: Eastland Disaster Relief, American Red Cross, 1915–1918: After the Capsizing of the Steamer "Eastland" in the Chicago River, July 24, 1915 to Completion of Relief Work. Final Report, Eastland Disaster Relief Committee, Chicago Chapter, American Red Cross, 1918, 11.

"unconscious harmony among those who": J. Byron Deacon, *Disasters and the American Red Cross in Disaster Relief* (New York: Russell Sage Foundation, 1918), 15.

"Ah, poor soul": "Picture of the Rescue Scene," *Palatine (IL) Enterprise,* July 30, 1915.

firemen tried in vain to: "Detective Proves Hero of Disaster by Saving 150 Trapped in Hull," *Washington Times,* July 25, 1915.

the water was cleared of: "Lake Boat Capsizes at Her Dock with 2,500 Aboard," *Pittsburgh Post-Gazette*, July 25, 1915.

"Tell them to send over": Repa, "Experiences of a Hawthorne Nurse."

trapped in a pit: Charles Kelly, letter to a friend, July 1915.

"Here! Stop that! You'll spoil the": "Stop! You'll Spoil the Boat," *Washington Herald*, July 25, 1915.

"Arrest that man and every": "Stop! You'll Spoil the Boat," *Washington Herald*, July 25, 1915.

"There didn't seem to be": Goyette, "What the Survivors Tell."

"How do you feel?": Goyette, "What the Survivors Tell."

"Pretty good, but I can't": Goyette, "What the Survivors Tell."

"Gangway! Gangway!": "Picture of the Rescue Scene," *Palatine (IL) Enterprise*, July 30, 1915.

"Isn't there some building where": Repa, "Experiences of a Hawthorne Nurse."

was taken alive from the: "Live Infant Is Rescued," *Los Angeles Times*, July 25, 1915.

"My God, it's Helen!": Repa, "Experiences of a Hawthorne Nurse."

"weighed down by lead-soled": "The History: Professional Divers," Eastland Disaster Historical Society, www.eastlanddisaster .org/history/professional-divers.

CHAPTER 8: EIGHTY-FIVE IN EACH ROW

"while tender hands, composed their": Ernest P. Bicknell, "The Eastland Disaster: An Incredible Tragedy in the Heart of Chicago," *American Red Cross Magazine*, January 1915.

"dumb horror in [her] wide": "Greatest of All Marine Disasters," *Charlotte (NC) News*, July 25, 1915.

"In the name of God": "Coroner Admits Tragic Throng to Huge Morgue," *Chicago Sunday Tribune*, July 25, 1915.

"Mothers, sisters, and daughters walked": "Coroner Admits Tragic Throng to Huge Morgue," *Chicago Sunday Tribune*, July 25, 1915.

The rubber stamp read: DROWNED: Hilton, *Eastland*, 109.

"Dear Mother, I am about": "Mad Scenes at Death's Post Office," *Chicago Examiner*, July 26, 1915.

Unidentified Dead: Chicago Tribune, July 27, 1915. This entry lists Number 396 as wearing a white suit. Several other newspaper articles refer to a brown suit that Willie Novotny was wearing when identified. It was not uncommon for incorrect information to be reported in the hours and days following this disaster.

"Little Feller": "2,000 to Mourn Little Feller," *Chicago Examiner*, July 31, 1915.

CHAPTER 9: BURIED MEMORIES

"You cry, too": "Cicero Streets Crowded with Funerals," *Chicago Day Book*, July 28, 1915.

It took two men four: Wachholz, *Eastland Disaster*, 70.

Kolin Avenue, a small street: "Every Kolin Home Loses Loved One," *Decatur (IL) Herald*, July 25, 1915.

called a funeral crepe: Emily Post, *Etiquette in Society, in Business, in Politics and at Home* (New York: Skyhorse, 2017), 433.

More than 6,000 wreaths and: "Shortage of Hearses as Hundreds of Wreck Victims Are Buried in Rain," *Los Angeles Evening Herald*, July 28, 1915.

"You might close your eyes": Charles Kelly, letter to a friend, July 1915.

"I want nothing but my babies": "Burial of the Dead Only Begins Tragedy for Hundreds of Bereaved," *Chicago Day Book*, July 27, 1915.

"To the President": Orrin E. Anderson, "From a Little Friend in Chicago," *Western Electric News*, August 1915.

White-garbed girls marched alongside: "Girlfriends of Victims Drenched as they March from Homes to Graves," *Chicago Examiner*, July 29, 1915.

"The little chap struck at": "Chums Identify Little Feller," *Chicago Examiner*, July 30, 1915.

Fifteen-year-old May Taylor: "Fifteen Cents for Flowers," *Lansing State Journal*, July 30, 1915.

"braved the horrors of the": "Chums Identify Little Feller," *Chicago Examiner*, July 30, 1915.

"That's him—Willie! said Frank": "Little Feller Now Has a Name," *Chicago Tribune*, July 30, 1915.

"If it's Willie, he's got": "Little Feller Now Has a Name," *Chicago Examiner*, July 30, 1915.

"stood outside the death room": "2,000 to Mourn Little Feller," *Chicago Examiner*, July 31, 1915.

"Chicago wants not revenge, but": "Little Feller Gets Homage of All Chicagoans," *Chicago Daily Tribune*, August 1, 1915.

"Kde Domov Muj": Joseph Mach Sr., "Catastophe on the Chicago River," *Amerikan Kalendár*, 1916.

100 children from the Bohemian: "2,000 to Mourn Little Feller," *Chicago Examiner*, July 30, 1915.

EPILOGUE

"When the Eastland was built": Judge Sessions, "Eastland was Built to Carry 500," *Detroit Free Press*, January 23, 1916.

"conspiracy to operate an unsafe": "The History Criminal Trial," Eastland Disaster Historical Society, www.eastlanddisaster.org/history/criminal-trial.

"I had no way of": "Eastland Never Tested," *New York Times*, January 23, 1916.

"The boat slid into the": "Eastland Never Tested," *New York Times*, January 23, 1916.

BIBLIOGRAPHY

———— . ————

BOOKS

Adams, Stephen B., and Orville R. Butler. *Manufacturing the Future: A History of Western Electric*. Cambridge: Cambridge University Press, 1999.

Bonansinga, Jay R. *The Sinking of the Eastland: America's Forgotten Tragedy*. New York: Citadel, 2004.

Deacon, J. Byron. *Disasters and the American Red Cross in Disaster Relief*. New York: Russell Sage Foundation, 1918.

Hilton, George Woodman. *Eastland: Legacy of the Titanic*. Stanford, CA: Stanford University Press, 1995.

McCarthy, Michael. *Ashes Under Water: The SS Eastland and the Shipwreck That Shook America*. Guilford, CT: Lyons, 2014.

Mitts, Dorothy Marie. *That Noble Country: The Romance of the St. Clair River Region*. Philadelphia: Dorrance, 1968.

Post, Emily. *Etiquette in Society, in Business, in Politics and at Home*. New York: Skyhorse, 2017.

Wachholz, Ted. *The Eastland Disaster*. Charleston, SC: Arcadia, 2005.

NEWSPAPERS ARTICLES, MAGAZINES, NEWS WIRE DISPATCHES

A.H. "Vacation Thoughts and Suggestions." *Western Electric News*, June 1913.

Anderson, Orrin E. "From a Little Friend in Chicago." *Western Electric News*, August 1915.

Babcock, Harlan E. "Harley Babcock Escaped Eastland—Tells How." *Republican-Northwestern* (Belvidere, IL), July 27, 1915.

Bicknell, Ernest P. "The Eastland Disaster: An Incredible Tragedy in the Heart of Chicago." *American Red Cross Magazine*, January 1915.

Burlington (VT) Weekly Free Press. "Drowned in Chicago Disaster." July 29, 1915.

Charlotte (NC) News. "Greatest of All Marine Disasters." July 25, 1915.

Chicago Daily Tribune. "'Little Feller' Gets Homage of All Chicagoans." August 1, 1915.

Chicago Daily Tribune. "Scare Onboard a Steamer." July 18, 1904.

Chicago Day Book. "Burial of the Dead Only Begins Tragedy for Hundreds of Bereaved." July 27, 1915.

Chicago Day Book. "Cicero Streets Crowded with Funerals." July 28, 1915.

Chicago Day Book. "Responsibility of Western Electric in Eastland Horror." July 26, 1915.

Chicago Examiner. "2,000 to Mourn Little Feller." July 31, 1915.

Chicago Examiner. "Chums Identify Little Feller." July 30, 1915.

Chicago Examiner. "Girlfriends of Victims Drenched as they March from Homes to Graves." July 29, 1915.

Chicago Examiner. "Mad Scenes at Death's Post Office." July 26, 1915.

Chicago Sunday Tribune. "Coroner Admits Tragic Throng to Huge Morgue." July 25, 1915.

Chicago Tribune. "Little Feller Now Has a Name." July 30, 1915.

Chicago Tribune. "Unidentified Dead." July 27, 1915.

Cross, Wilbur. "Disaster at the Dock." *Coronet*, September 1957. 133–137.

Decatur (IL) Herald. "Every Kolin Home Loses Loved One." July 25, 1915.

F.S. "Forced to Buy Tickets." *Chicago Day Book*, July 29, 1915.

Goyette, George A. "What the Survivors Tell." *Western Electric News*, August 1915.

Hicks, R. W. "The Eastland Disaster." *Safety Engineering: Prevention of Needless Waste by Fires and Accidents* 30 (July–December 1915): 101–108.

Kelly, C. C. "What the Survivors Tell." *Western Electric News*, August 1915.

Lansing State Journal. "Fifteen Cents for Flowers." July 30, 1915.

Los Angeles Evening Herald. "Shortage of Hearses as Hundreds of Wreck Victims Are Buried in Rain." July 28, 1915.

Los Angeles Times. "Live Infant Is Rescued." July 25, 1915.

Mach, Josef, Sr. "Catastrophe on the Chicago River." *Amerikan Kalendár*, 1916.

New York Times. "Eastland Never Tested." January 23, 1916.

Palatine (IL) Enterprise. "Picture of the Rescue Scene." July 30, 1915.

Pittsburgh Post-Gazette. "Human Chain Saves Three." July 25, 1915.

Pittsburgh, Post-Gazette. "Lake Boat Capsizes at her Dock with 2,500 Aboard." July 25, 1915.

Repa, Helen. "The Experiences of a Hawthorne Nurse." *Western Electric News*, August 1915.

Sessions, Judge. "Eastland Was Built to Carry." *Detroit Free Press*, January 23, 1916.

Washington Herald. "Stop! You'll Spoil the Boat." July 25, 1915.

Washington Times. "Detective Proves Hero of Disaster by Saving 150 Trapped in Hull." July 24, 1915.

Weber, Austin. "The Hawthorne Works." *Assembly Magazine*, August 1, 2002. www.assemblymag.com/articles/88188-the-hawthorne-works.

Wendemuth, Lillian M. "Our Women and Their Work." *Western Electric News*, April 1913.

Western Electric News. "A Date Never to Be Forgotten." April 1913.

OFFICIAL REPORTS

Eastland Disaster Relief, American Red Cross, 1915–1918: After the Capsizing of the Steamer "Eastland" in the Chicago River, July 24, 1915 to Completion of Relief Work. Final Report, Eastland Disaster Relief Committee, Chicago Chapter, American Red Cross, 1918.

Investigation of Accident to the Steamer "Eastland": Chicago Ill., July 24 to August 5, 1915, Printed for the use of the Committee on Merchant Marine and Fisheries. 64th Congress (1916).

Transcript of the Testimony: Before the Coroner's Jury, July 24, 25, 26, 27, 28, 29, on the Body of Kate Austin and All Others Lost by the Overturning of the Excursion Steamer Eastland While Tied to the Dock at Clark and S. Water Streets in the City of Chicago, July 24, 1915.

WEBSITES

Eastland Disaster Historical Society, www.eastlanddisaster.org.

PERSONAL INTERVIEWS

Wachholz, Barbara and Ted. Interview by author. November 11, 2014; March 4, 2016.

LETTERS

Kelly, Charles, to a friend, July 1915. This letter was made available to the author as a courtesy by the Eastland Disaster Historical Society.

IMAGE CREDITS

—— . ——

Page 23: Author's collection
Page 26: Image illustrated by Thomas W. Reid III
Page 32–33: Library of Congress LC-D4-22668
Page 40–41: Library of Congress LC-D418-68295
Page 46: C. Patrick Labadie Collection/Thunder Bay National Marine Sanctuary 48708.48732
Page 55: Lindsey Cleworth Schauer
Page 61: Author's collection
Page 64–65: Library of Congress LC-USZ62-126620
Page 72–73: Chicago History Museum ICHi-30727; Jun Fujita, photographer
Page 84: Chicago History Museum ICHi-40121; Jun Fujita, photographer
Page 87: *Chicago Daily News* negatives collection, DN-006937; Chicago History Museum
Page 96: Chicago History Museum ICHi-30729; Jun Fujita, photographer
Page 102: Chicago History Museum ICHi-40122; Jun Fujita, photographer
Page 113: *Chicago Daily News* negatives collection, DN-0064961; Chicago History Museum
Page 115: Author's collection
Page 120: Author's collection
Page 121: Author's collection
Page 128–129: National Archives at Chicago: Record Group 21. Exhibit #24, U.S. District Court for the Southern (Grand Rapids) Division of the Western District of Michigan. 6/19/1878— Criminal Court Case 1628, *United States vs. William H. Hull, George T. Arnold, Harry Pedersen, Joseph M. Erickson, Robert Reid, and Charles Eckliff*
Page 133: Author's collection

INDEX

——·——